Anthropology for a Small Planet:

Culture and Community in a Global Environment

second edition

Anthropology for a Small Planet:

Culture and Community in a Global Environment

second edition

Edited by
Charles R. Menzies
Anthony Marcus

New Proposals Publishing
Vancouver
2013

Copyright © 2013 New Proposals Publishing

Copyright of articles remains with the authors.

New Proposals Publishing
6303 NW Marine Drive
Vancouver BC
V6T 1Z1

First edition published 1996 by Brandywine Press, St. James, New York. ISBN 1-881-089-86-X.

Edited by Charles R. Menzies and Anthony Marcus

Design and Layout by Kenneth Campbell

Printed in Canada by Friesens

Cover: No Olympics on Stolen Native Land, Vancouver 2010. Jamie Cooper photograph.

Library and Archives Canada Cataloguing in Publication
    Anthropology for a small planet : culture and community in a global environment / [edited by Charles R. Menzies and Anthony Marcus]. -- 2nd ed.

Includes bibliographical references.
ISBN 978-0-9917578-0-0

    1. Ethnology. 2. Ethnology--Case studies. I. Menzies, Charles R. II. Marcus, Anthony, 1963-

GN316.A56 2013   306   C2012-907272-9

Contents

Preface

Research – meeting people, talking to them, working with them, interviewing them – is what anthropology is all about. Socio-cultural anthropology draws upon friend-like relationships to reconstruct detailed understandings of small groups of people. Whereas survey research, for example, paints broad brush pictures of large groups of people, anthropology focuses on long term relationships. The survey approach might give one a lot of superficial details about a large number of people. Anthropology, however, gives one rich detail about a small number of people. Both views have advantages, but for me I am more inclined toward long-term relationships than the one-night stand of large-scale surveys.

At the heart of the anthropological endeavour is a desire to make sense of our world through long-term, intimate social relations. There are certainly many types of anthropological research. Nonetheless, and despite all of our differences, all anthropologists share a desire to learn about real people and to apply the knowledge we gain to making our common world a better place for all.

This edited collection had its roots in a circle of friends and colleagues studying at the City University of New York's Graduate Center in the mid-1990s. As we were making the transition from students to teachers we felt the desire to have teachable case studies that dealt with real problems that our mostly urban students would relate to. Anthony Marcus, the editor of the first edition of *Anthropology for a Small Planet*, took the initiative and organized the first volume. Marcus wanted clearly written and engaging articles that demonstrated anthropology in action.

Between the publication of the first and second editions Marcus and Menzies, in collaboration with Katherine McCaffrey and Sharon Roseman, founded the journal *New Proposals*. The journal is an attempt to explore issues, ideas, and problems that lie at the intersection between the academic discipline of social anthropology and the body of thought and political practice that has constituted Marxism over the last 150 years. The University of British Columbia in Vancouver, Canada hosts our journal, which is an experiment in open access publication.

The second edition of *Anthropology for a Small Planet* blends together four of the original articles with five published in *New Proposals*. Each essay was selected for its relevance for learning about how to do anthropology that makes a difference in our world. Too often our academic studies focus on pointing out everything that is wrong but ignore what can actually be done or deny the reality of the world that most people live in. That's not the case here. This collection of case studies teaches by example. Yes, the reader will see authors engage in critique, but most importantly our authors show how to conduct anthropology that makes a difference.

The first set of essays focus on the intersection between race and nationality. The second set of essays explores the intersection of social identity, belief, and inequality. The final set of essays documents the possibilities for an engaged anthropology rooted in a social justice paradigm.

Charles R. Menzies

INTRODUCTION
A SMALL PLANET

Katherine McCaffrey and Anthony Marcus

Everyone knows that we live in a global world. Today, children with inexpensive personal computers send and receive messages across the globe in seconds using technology that was once only available to scientists and statesmen. Indigenous peoples in the most remote villages in the high mountains of South America gather around a village television set to watch Glee and CSI. Colombian peasants without running water in their homes watch CNBC financial news to decide when to sell their coffee harvest, while high school janitors in Little Rock, Arkansas, keep track of the Singapore stock market to decide when they can retire. The defeat of industrial strikes and protests in Korea in 1980 and the collapse of the Mexican peso in 1982 by lowering wages in Korea and Mexico lead companies to shift factories around the world and decrease workers' living standards in the United States. The actions of people we will never meet on the other side of the planet change our everyday lives.

Anthropology has always taken all of humankind as its subject and the whole world as its laboratory to study what it means to be human and live in groups with other humans. For anthropologists, the "new globalism" is but one new chapter in a much longer story of human development, part of the epic tale of one species, *Homo sapiens*, which has been engaging in long-distance travel and trade, war, intermarriage, and cross-cultural contact since the dawn of modern humans nearly 100,000 years ago. These external connections and outside influences that transform local lives have been the rule of human history rather than the exception.

On this small planet where the actions of people across the globe have a profound influence on our daily lives and our futures, we must understand something about the lives of people across the oceans and the way they view the world, if we are to successfully interact with them. This is the mission of anthropology: to understand the differences and similarities, the understandings, expectations, and desires of peoples living in a wide variety of conditions, circumstances, and environments.

This introductory essay underscores why anthropology is well-suited to make sense of the crazy quilt of human existence. It looks at the discipline's origins as "world anthropology" and the way in which contemporary political and economic processes, in particular the events and aftermath of World War II, have reinforced this mission. It considers the volume's articles, written from fieldsites as different as Palestine and Cuba; covering actors as varied as American minutemen, African refugees in Israel, and Canadian fishers; and shows how they are informed by a recognition of the broader forces of politics and economics that bind humans together in a complex weave.

Anthropology Confronts Globalism: Early Trends

Anthropology, as a social science, developed in nineteenth-century Europe as it was being fundamentally transformed by the rise of capitalism and the industrial revolution. Anthropology and the other modern social sciences such as sociology, economics, and political science, developed in response to the sense of uncertainty and social dislocation caused by these profound political and economic changes. Anthropology, however, more than any other social science, was global in its vision. Its very name identified it as the "science of humanity." It set out to explain the world that capitalism had made smaller, trying to bring some sense of order to the chaos that is human existence (see Wolf 1982).

At its origin, anthropology was concerned mainly with the study of non-Western peoples. Since the days of Columbus, Western travellers and missionaries encountered people vastly different from those of European extraction. Westerners told wide-eyed stories of two-headed beings, flesh-eating savages, and naked wildmen running in the bush. At the moment of anthropology's birth in the nineteenth century, however, European nations were expanding across the globe, establishing colonial empires in which they could secure resources and establish new markets. This required Westerners to develop new relationships – however unequal – with these peoples often described as so exotic.

Early anthropologists, responding to Europeans' need to understand their colonies, first sought to explain the evolution of culture on a worldwide scale. Edward

Burnett Tyior (1832-1917) and Lewis Henry Morgan (1818-1881), the key thinkers on this topic, theorized that all of the varying peoples of the world belonged to one race, humanity, and that social and cultural differences could be explained by charting human development into different sequential stages: savagery, barbarism, and civilization. There were gross limitations to their theorizing: they viewed human history as a linear path of progress, in which European social organization represented the pinnacle of progress and all other societies were just underdeveloped versions of Victorian England. But unlike other thinkers who searched for racial explanations of cultural difference, Morgan and Tylor established the mainstream of anthropology: the idea that all people, however different and seemingly strange, nonetheless belonged to one race: humanity. The next generation of anthropologists soon made a name for themselves by going out into the world and describing life as they actually saw it. Ethnography, the art of describing culture, became the hallmark and distinguishing feature of the discipline. Often but not always studying colonial subjects of the anthropologist's home country, they went to small villages in distant lands, learned new languages, and recorded the lifeways of peoples vastly different from themselves. Working on a local level, with a commitment to seeing life holistically through the eyes of the people they studied, anthropologists gained intimate understandings of individual cultures and rich descriptions of local life. But theorists often had a hard time relating these community studies to a broader schema, to an understanding of how this one village or society, was part of a larger picture – a region, a nation, the world.

Furthermore, ethnographers too often neglected history. Even though many of the places anthropologists studied were colonies, enmeshed in a complex and changing relationship with imperial powers, these small villages were often depicted as outside the currents of human history. This depiction of cultures as essentially isolated and static became increasingly difficult to maintain in the aftermath of World War II.

World War Two and Beyond: Towards a Small Planet

World War II fundamentally reoriented anthropology towards its origins as a world science. The war moved people around the globe on an unprecedented scale. Fought on every continent, the war linked previously ignored sections of the globe through new military communications networks, supply lines, and political interdependencies. The seemingly timeless and isolated tribes and village communities that anthropologists had studied before the war were now permanently transformed. After the war, when anthropologists returned to the fieldsites of the colonial world, they found everywhere the direct effects of outside forces: whole villages wiped away by advancing armies, abandoned military hardware, electric generators for field stations, children of long gone soldiers bearing their father's names, international bankers and U.S. and UN advisers attempting to organize the reconstruction and still unresolved conflicts generated by the war.

As the pre-World War II colonial world disappeared, former colonial peoples sought to rule themselves in their own nations. In places like China, Africa, Korea, and Vietnam locally-based militias composed of ordinary citizens found themselves victorious over fascism and asked why they should continue to allow colonial powers like France and England to dominate them. Often liberation from the colonial powers meant overthrowing their own indigenous rulers, tied to the colonial system. Worker and peasant militias, led by popular local leaders like Mao Zedong in China, Kim Il Sung in Korea, Ho Chi Minh in Vietnam, and Marshal Tito in Yugoslavia fought civil wars against the traditional rulers of their countries.

On every continent people confronted a bipolar world divided between the communist camp of the Soviet Union and a capitalist camp led by the United States. They struggled over what kind of a society they would build and which camp they would join. Nations in both camps suffered with the changing position of their "superpower" patron – as the Marcus article on Cuba demonstrates. Groups unable to consolidate strong nation-states with the direct support of one of the two "superpowers" were likely to be left out in the cold, fleeing their homes as refugees or living as foreigners in their own nations as the Palestinians discussed in Sawalha articles.

In sum, out of the global cataclysm that was World War II came our present world: a much smaller, more interdependent planet where events in one place profoundly influence people's lives many thousands of miles away. Anthropologists now had to study individual cultures and societies as part of a political and economic system that was constantly creating and re-creating people's very sense of themselves.

Anthropology in a Global Environment: Theoretical Approaches

Anthropology in the postwar United States increasingly focused on issues of cultural change and "modernization." (Vincent 1990:225-307). Robert Redfield studied how modern processes of conquest, urbanization, and migration transformed peasant society into urban society (see Redfield 1960). Another example, Anthony Wallace treated the Ghost Dance of the Plains Indians as a cultural response to a colonial encounter (Wallace 1956). Julian Steward's People of Puerto Rico project represented an effort to move from studying small cultures and microcosms to the study of complex, class-structured colonial society (Steward 1956). Anthropologists, once identified solely with the study of "traditional" peoples and ways of life took up the study of rural proletarians and the urban poor (Mintz 1960, Lewis 1966).

The most significant development in anthropological thinking of the postwar period, however, occurred in the context of anti-colonial revolt in what came to be called the Third World, particularly the revolutions in China and Cuba. Marxism entered the academy. Like anthropology, Marxism was holistic and global in its approach. It brought a focus on power, history, and worldwide political and economic process to anthropological theory and practice.

As a result of the focus on power, anthropology confronted its own complicity in the spread and maintenance of imperialism and revamped both its methods and theories (see Hymes 1969). Marxism brought a focus on history to the discipline. Anthropologists were encouraged to contextualize societies, individuals, and behaviour in light of historical events and processes (Smith 1984). Wars and acts of resistance and the contemporary politics of Third-World peasantry became important topics of inquiry (Wolf 1969, Scott 1976). The poverty and quaintness that was often depicted as part of the traditional way of life was shown often to be the result of exploitation by and resistance to the West (Worseley 1957, Wolf 1982, Wilmsen 1989).

Significantly, Marxism also functioned on the practical level. A key element of Marxist theory was its belief in the unity of theory and practice. Marxism encouraged anthropologists to address issues that would not just remain in the academy, but contribute to the achievement of a more just world. Thus Marxist anthropologists took up issues such as the subordination of women (Etienne and Leacock 1980, Nash and Safa 1974), racial and ethnic conflict and inequality (Mencher 1974), and colonialism (Wessman 1981) as part of a vision of not just describing the world, but changing it.

Culture and Community in a Global Environment

The collapse of the Soviet Union in 1989-1991 and the triumph of capitalism have forced anthropologists to ask new questions about human life and culture as they grapple with the social and cultural implications of the rapidly accelerated pace of globalization. More and more, anthropologists feel uneasy about their ability to make sense of the world. Some even speak of a "crisis of representation," in which old ways of thinking are increasingly inadequate to describe a world in transition (see Marcus and Fischer 1986).

These essays are part of a trend in anthropology that is global in vision, that links local cultural forms to broader political and economic processes. The essays confront contemporary human problems – such as racism, poverty, inequality – and draw upon anthropology's tradition of holism to make sense of cultural particularities. This world that is growing smaller is also growing more economically and politically polarized. Multinational textile factories and electronic assembly plants employ thousands of men, women, and children in Asia, Latin America, and the Caribbean who work for meager wages to produce clothing and luxury items for a largely Western consumer market. The oil shock of 1973-75, then the debt crisis of 1982 clearly revealed both the rapid rate of globalization and the increasing inequities between the First World and the Third World, the North and South. The crisis showed that as governments and peoples were more directly drawn into the international economic system, they were incorporated unevenly and unequally.

Globalization is not only political and economic, but cultural. In South India, a rickshaw wallah blares a Michael Jackson cassette, while in Iran, a woman in a chodor sneaks a Marlboro cigarette. In a world where emblems of Western society seem ubiquitous, camera-clicking tourists and travellers disenchanted with Western ways set forth to remote corners of the globe, searching for more authentic peoples and timeless cultures.

A common theme in many of these essays is the relationship between economic and social forms. The new international economy is producing a variety of cultural responses on a global scale. In Cuba, Marcus argues that the deterioration of the socialist state threatens the social status of Afro-Cubans. In Dominica shifting positions in the global economy contribute to rising local poverty in which American medical aid appears as yet another form of colonialism. As Menzies points out, there is no simple, one-to-one correspondence between economics and social forms. In Canada, Menzies examines the ways in which two men of essentially similar social origin are assigned different racial identities as "White" and " Indian," and how differently they therefore fit into a capitalist production that relies upon a racially segregated workforce for its perpetuation.

Several essays of the book point to the powerful effect of global forces on the lives of ordinary people as well as how they mediate such pressures. In Yaron's article the economic disruption of sub-Saharan Africa contributes to an influx of refugees in Israel. Sawalha presents Palestinians forging a new identity in opposition to the forces that try to eliminate or assimilate them. Chin shows African-American girls in New Haven, Connecticut, transforming mass-produced symbols into ones with distinct, local cultural meaning.

New Identities in a Changed World

Rather than fearing the loss of culture, community, and self in today's world, many anthropologists celebrate the global consciousness that is currently developing. While we are disturbed by the terrible conflicts, fratricidal wars, and increased economic inequality that is currently ravaging the globe, we see tremendous possibilities in this new, smaller world. We close this collection with two articles that highlight the applied role of anthropologists in making our world a better place for all. As anthropologists and citizens of the world we draw on our discipline's commitment to respect for cultural difference and an integrated and global view of humanity. Only with such a larger analysis and vision can we build a world where people are not just strangers across oceans, but neighbours in a global world.

References

Bohannan, Paul and Mark Glazer

    1988   High Points in Anthropology. New York: Alfred A. Knopf.

Etienne, Mona and Eleanor Leacock, eds.

    1980   Women and Colonization: Anthropological Perspectives. New York: Bergin and Garvey/Praeger.

Hymes, Dell, ed.

    1969   Reinventing Anthropology. New York: Pantheon.

Lewis, Oscar

    1966   La Vida: A Puerto Rican Family in the Culture of Poverty in San Juan and New York. New York: Random House.

Marcus, George and Michael Fischer

    1986   Anthropology as Cultural Critique: An Experimental Moment in the Human Sciences. Chicago University of Chicago Press.

Mencher, Joan P.

    1974   The Caste System Upside Down or the Not-So-Mysterious East. Current Anthropology 15:469-494.

Mintz, Sidney

    1960   Worker in the Cane: A Puerto Rican Life History. New Haven, Yale University Press.

Nash, June and Helen Safa, eds.

    1976   Sex and Class in Latin America. New York: Praeger.

Redfield, Robert
  1960   The Little Community and Peasant Society and Culture. Chicago: University
          of Chicago Press.
Scott, James
  1976   The Moral Economy of the Peasant: Rebellion and Subsistence in Southeast
          Asia. New Haven. Yale University Press.
Smith, Carol
  1984   Local history in global context. Comparative Studies in Society and History
          26:193-228.
Steward, Julian, ed.
  1956   The People of Puerto Rico: A Study in Social Anthropology. Urbana:
          University of Illinois Press.
Vincent, Joan
  1990   Anthropology and Politics. Tucson: University of Arizona Press.
Wallace, Anthony
  1956   Revitalization movements. American Anthropologist 58:264-281.
Wessman, James
  1981   Anthropology and Marxism. Cambridge, Mass: Schenkman.
Wilmsen, E.
  1989   Land Filled With Flies: A Political Economy of the Kalahari. Chicago:
          University of Chicago Press.
Wolf, Eric R.
  1982   Europe and the People Without History. Berkeley: University of California
          Press.
  1969   Peasant Wars of the Twentieth Century. New York: Harper Row.
Worsley P.
  1957   The Trumpet Shall Sound: A Study of "Cargo" Cults in Melanesia. London:
          MacGibbon and Kee.

Part One
Race and Nationality

IDENTITY, THE SELF, AND THE OTHER
In a Poor Neighborhood in East Amman

Aseel Sawalha

Although I have the Jordanian passport, and I lived in this same area(Wadi al-Rimam)
since 1948, and my 8 sons and daughters were born here, I am not Jordanian and I will
never become so. I and my sons and daughters are Palestinian refugees in Jordan. I f I
was given a Palace in Amman I won't take it, I will stay with other refugees.

Abu Naser, fifty-seven-year-old Palestinian refugee

Introduction

In 1948, almost four hundred Arab villages were demolished by the Israelis. The
Palestinians, as a consequence, sought refuge in surrounding Arab countries. Since
then Palestinians have not been allowed to re-enter the land of their birth, forming a diaspora which today comprises approximately four million people scattered
throughout the world (Morris 1986; Said 1983, 1986).

Here I will describe the different forms of identity among Palestinian refugees
in a poor neighbourhood in East Amman, Jordan. The interaction and performances
of the refugees in daily life are to a large extent shaped by the way they conceive of
their pasts, and by the way other people address them in various contexts. The various
ways by which people identify themselves and are identified by others include their
being members of a specific household or family; residents of a certain neighbourhood in Amman; being of a specific village or town in Palestine of 1948; or simply as
Palestinian refugees in Jordan. In what follows I will present the complex interaction

between two places (exile and homeland) in relation to the past and the present and as they are manifested in everyday practices.

Both Palestinian people and many Arab writers refer to the cataclysmic period beginning in 1948 as *Al-Nakba*, (the Catastrophe or the Disaster), a term that evokes loss, alienation, tragedy, and betrayal (Peteet 1991; Bisharat 1994). The *Nakba* year, 1948, has played a central role in the construction of Palestinian historical consciousness and identity. Palestinians in the refugee camps periodize their existence around the *Nakba* and consider it a cutting point in their history. They usually describe the period prior to 1948 as one of stability and happiness, while the "post-*Nakba*" stage is referred to as the starting point of a series of displacements, miseries, bad luck, and suffering.

Warda's Life

The story of Warda, a thirty-four-year-old mother of five children living in a one room apartment in a Palestinian refugee camp in Amman offers a representative history of displacement:[1]

My father's family was living in a village on the Mediterranean coast of Palestine. They were farmers and they owned large farms of orange trees and olives. In 1948 they were forced out of their home village as all the Palestinians after the Israeli occupation of Palestine. My father's family settled in a refugee camp near Jerusalem. Ten years later, after they lost hope of going back to their home village, my father married my mother who is his relative from the same village of origin. I was born in the refugee camp in 1961. In 1967 we fled to Jordan after the second Arab-Israeli war and the occupation of the rest of Palestine by the Israelis. We stayed in this same refugee camp where there are families from our village. A few days after we came to Jordan my father went back to Palestine with the Palestinian resistance movement, and never came back. He was killed by the Israelis on the borders while he was crossing Jordan river.

My mother took the responsibility of bringing up me and my sister and brother; my oldest brother was 9 years old. [Warda pointed to her children saying that she and her brothers were at the same age as her children.] We did not go to school when we first came to Jordan, because we . . . did not have any money; we lost everything, the house, the money and the father. A few years later my mother worked as a cleaning lady at one of the UNRWA schools. My brother and sister went to school but I did not; I had to stay home to do the housework and to take

---

1   In the following, the major incidents in Warda's life are arranged chronologically for the sake of analysis. This does not mean that this is the way she put them according to their priority in her own life.

care of my younger brothers. I missed going to school, when I saw the boys and girls of my age, going and coming back from the school I was crying all the time. Because of this I will do anything to keep my children at school.

I got married when I was 18. My husband was a Palestinian refugee from a village close to my village in Palestine; he was working in Kuwait. I was sent to him to Kuwait with some of his relatives. I lived a relatively good life in Kuwait with my husband who was working as a driver. I thought that marriage will put an end to the days of poverty and misery, but during the Gulf war in 1991, we have to come back to Jordan without any money and without my husband. My husband died in a car accident during the war. We had some savings in a bank in Kuwait but because of the war we were unable to get any of it. I rented a truck to move my children and some furniture. At the beginning I stayed with my husband's family in this refugee camp, but a few months later the problems started after I spent all the money that I had in Kuwait. When the problems started between me and my in-laws I moved with my children to live with my brother and his wife and children, but their two-room house is not enough for me, my children and my mother. I rented this room and my mother moved with us, because the people around us will talk negatively about me as a young widow living on my own.

The experience of displacement and the loss of home have given the Palestinians a marked identity among other Arabs in the region. After they were forced out of their country, Palestinians started to identify themselves and be identified according to where they live in exile: the Palestinians of Jordan, the Palestinians of Lebanon, the Palestinians of Syria, and so on. In Jordan, since 1948, Palestinians of peasant origins who were forced to leave their villages have lived in refugee camps run by UNRWA (United Nations Relief and Works Agency) in Jordan and have tended to cluster in groups composed of refugees from neighbouring villages in Palestine. Many families who were not able to gain access to UNRWA havens established squatter areas close to the camps of their relatives.

Representations of Home in Refugee's Daily Life

This study is based on six months of field research in Wadi al-Rimam, a Palestinian squatter neighborhood in Amman.[2] The boundaries of the studied community are as ambiguous as the identities of its inhabitants. Wadi al-Rimam is a valley located between two mountains, Jabal al-Taj and Jabal al-Nasir in the centre of the city

---

2   I chose the area for this specific research after participating in a survey on children and health in poor neighbourhoods in Amman with Jocelyn DeJong.

of Amman. The houses in these areas are mostly owned or rented by Palestinian refugees who left in 1948. Close to Wadi al-Rimam is Hayy al-Tafayleh and Hayy al-Mma'aniya, whose residents are mostly from the towns of Tafeela and Ma'an in Southern Jordan who are not Palestinians. Wadi al-Rimam is surrounded on two sides by a wall made of cement, which separates it from the other two neighbourhoods. The people of the area do not know who built this wall, but besides its symbolic significance this wall limits Palestinians of Wadial-Rimam in their relations with residents of the neighbouring areas.

Wadi al-Rimam is known by a number of names. Its inhabitants call it Harat al-Mahasra after the village of Beit Mahseer, since the majority of the first inhabitants of this valley were from this particular Palestinian village located west of Jerusalem. Being one of the first villages to be completely destroyed by the Israelis in the 1948 war, its people were among the first to be expelled from Palestine and head to Jordan. The boundaries of Haratal-Mahasra are not well defined. Sometimes the term is used to refer only to the upper part of the valley, and at other times to the whole valley. Inhabitants of other areas of East Amman call this area Wadi al-Rimam, while many of the people who live in wealthy West Amman do not even know of its existence. The term Wadi al-Rimam literally means "the valley of dead animals," referring to the pre-1948 period when people in the surrounding areas used to throw their garbage and dead animals in this valley. Palestinian refugees often boast that they "developed" and changed the area. They state that they usually build and improve the places where they settle, and offer the example of the Gulf States. One of the people of Wadi al-Rimam asserted "we (Palestinians) leave our green fingerprints wherever we go. We changed this place from a valley of the dead to a valley full of life, as you see."

Administratively, the area is registered as Wadi al-Nasir or valley of victory. Generally speaking, the houses look very poor from the outside, and are clustered very close to each other. The upper part of this area contains about 150 households included in an urban upgrading development project. These houses are separated by narrow paved alleys not exceeding the width of one metre. A number of houses in this part are built of concrete, and some have two stories. The land on which these houses are built was sold to the residents by the Urban Development Department. In contrast, the lower part of the valley comprises about one hundred households which are not included in the project and lack basic services such as water, electricity, and sewerage. The houses here are poorer and smaller, are built mostly of mud and corrugated metal, and the alleys separating the houses are not paved. Nor do the people in this part have legal ownership.

Both the upper and the lower parts of Wadi al-Rimam are crowded and many people, especially women and children, are in the alleys during the daytime. A number of houses operate as small shops usually run by older women. Often, women sit in front of these shops engaged in food processing like cleaning lentils and rice, or knitting and embroidering. The children play most of the time outside the houses because the houses are so small.

In addition to the majority of the inhabitants who come from Beit Mahseer, there are also people from a number of villages located near Jerusalem as well as from Lydda and Ramleh, two Palestinian cities which were occupied in 1948. Peteet notes that "the majority of Palestinian refugees living in camps – in Lebanon – (70 to 80%), were small landowning peasants or sharecroppers" (1991:20). When these Palestinian peasants first came to Jordan, they settled, wherever possible, in villages where they had family affiliations. Sayigh (1979) in a study about Palestinian refugees in Lebanon stated that the camps were arranged to re-create the pre-1948 Palestine villages. Streets, alleys, shops and markets which sprouted in the camps were named for the villages and towns from which the residents came. Similarly, in Wadi al-Rimam place names frequently refer to the village of origin or to the strong hope of return and the sacrifice and struggle connected to that hope. Examples include, Al-Thawrah (the revolution), Al-Nasir (the victory), Al-Nidal (the struggle),and Al-'Awdah (the return). Examples of other names include Falasteen(Palestine), Al-Quds (Jerusalem) and Bab Al-Amoud (a neighborhood in Jerusalem).

Upon their arrival in Jordan, Palestinian refugees formed committees upon request from UNRWA and the Jordanian government to organize receiving United Nation's aid. These committees consist of one or two persons from each village, including the *mukhtar* or the former headman of the village of origin (Plascov 1981) who received official recognition from the Jordanian government. At the beginning, these committees apparently did not have a political role, but were limited to carrying out relief policies and mediating between the refugees, the Jordanian state,and the relief agencies. Each *mukhtar* was given a government stamp to provide proof of identity for the people of his village of origin which is required to get official papers. The *mukhtar* also plays a crucial role in solving problems among the people of his village of origin. Later their activities expanded and their numbers increased. Now there are committees for almost each village and for most large families. Many of these committees and organizations are registered in Jordan as *rawabit* (organizations). Members of these organizations either meet in a rented place or some built their own space from designated contributions from members of the village of origin.

All males from the village of origin who are over the age of eighteen pay a yearly membership fee. These committees are based upon the place of origin in Palestine regardless of the place of residence in diaspora. It must be noted that membership in these committees is restricted to men.

Currently, these committees help in collecting financial aid for families in crises, when the male provider of a family dies. Members of the *rawabit* also intervene in solving problems and conflicts at different levels as in the cases of fights with and accidents involving Jordanians or Palestinians from other villages. The *rawabit* also form a place for people from the same village to gather and exchange news, and provide a forum for younger people to meet the older generations. Since the houses of most of the Palestinian refugees are too small to perform ceremonies when the occasion arises, many weddings and funerals take place at the *rawabit*.

Refugees as an Identity

The transformation in the meaning and the uses of the word "refugee"illustrates the way Palestinian refugees identify themselves in different situations. The people of Wadi al-Rimam are all of Palestinian origin and have Jordanian citizenship; at the same time they have UN refugee status, as do most Palestinian refugees in Jordan. The closest Palestinian camp to this area is the Jabal al-Nasir, an UNRWA refugee camp which is inhabited by people from the same villages as Wadi al-Rimam. People of both areas have access to UNRWA services at the Jabal al-Nasir camp, such as the UNRWA schools and health and training centres.

Since the 1950s there has been a constant movement in and out of Wadi al-Rimam. The first Palestinian inhabitants of the area bought small mud houses roofed with metal sheets from the bedouins who used to come seasonally to the area with their animals. Gradually, their relatives and neighbours from the villages of origin in Palestine started to move to this area after they too faced problems in finding places to stay. The price of land was cheap compared to the prices in other areas, and it was close to the city centre where men used to look for work as daily labourers and women for domestic work. In 1967, after the occupation of the rest of Palestine by the Israelis, Palestinian *naziheen* (officially labelled as displaced) from the West Bank and Gaza also came to this area.[3] The majority of the newcomers in 1967 were relatives of older residents of the area either through kinship or marriage, or were from the same villages of origin. At the time I conducted my research in 1992, a number

---

3   Palestinian refugees from 1948 are known as *laji`een* (refugees) whereas those of 1967 are known as *naziheen* (displaced). This is in conformity with UN regulations which only recognize those who cross an international border as officially refugees.

of families forced to leave Kuwait or other Gulf countries after the 1991 Gulf war were looking to either buy or rent houses in the area. These people are called 'a'ideen (returnees). Most of these families – Warda is representative – either had kin in this area, or had grown up there before they went to the Gulf.

In Wadi al-Rimam, the sons of the three groups of refugees (laji'een 1948, naziheen 1967, and 'a'ideen 1991) either stay in the same housing unit after they marry in a separate room and share the kitchen and the bathroom, or they try to rent a house in the area. Those with better economic conditions because of education or a regular job, move outside to other neighbouring areas, mostly to Jabal Al-Taj or Jabal Al-Nasir. Immediately after moving, people usually stay in touch with their relatives in the valley, but gradually those who move away from the area reduce their participation in the activities of the valley to the displeasure of their relatives.

The Image of Home in Refugee's Daily Life

Memories of the former villages remain vivid in exile. When people feel upset about their daily problems in Jordan like unemployment, discrimination, or poverty they usually blame it on their status as exiles, and their immediate response is to remember 'ayyam al-'iz, 'ayyam li-blad (the days of happiness in the home-country). Rosemary Sayigh has written that Palestinian refugees in Beirut, Lebanon remembered living in their village as living in paradise (1979:10). Although people in Wadi al-Rimam romanticize their villages of origin, they still reflect the conflicts between people back home in some of the relations of the refugees in exile. For example one family refused to marry their daughter to a man from the same village because of a land dispute between their families in the town of origin.

When I asked people in Wadi al-Rimam where they were from, most did not refer to the place in which they presently live in Amman, especially if they did not own the house they inhabited, or if their economic situation was not good, or if non-Palestinians were present. The first response was to give the name of the village of origin in Palestine; usually they followed this with a comment that the village had been demolished by the Israelis; sometimes they would also volunteer the Hebrew name of the Israeli settlement established after the destruction of the village. Many of them complained of the bad economic situation in Jordan, and compared life as refugees to what life was once like when they lived in their own villages. They talked painfully about the experience of leaving the village of origin "al-qaryya al-asleyya," and the hopes of returning home.

Few Palestinian refugees in Jordan have had the opportunity of visiting their birthplace after they were forced out. Those who have always tell stories about what remains of their villages, and everyone transmits and retells the story in his or her own way. There is a constant fixation on certain symbols that still exist of the village. For example, they would say "the whole village has been converted by the Israelis into a farm for raising cows, and all of the houses were demolished, but the wall of the cemetery is still there," or "the *ma`thaneh* (the minaret) of the big mosque is lying on the edge of the valley." Others mention that the house of so and so is still there, and the school is renovated and re-used as a kindergarten, or a flower garden has taken the place of the village, but the fields of oranges and the olive trees remain.

Many families retain the keys to their homes that were demolished by the Israelis as symbols of their determination to return. Other families still have the official papers which show their ownership of houses and land in their former villages. They keep these with their official papers like the family card, UN refugee card, and passports. Some have asked those who had the opportunity to visit the villages of origin to bring them back some of the soil of Palestine.

After forty-four years of living away from their home villages, the Palestinians may have become "more used" to it and may have developed some adaptation strategies or a new "Palestinian culture and tradition in exile" (Said 1986). But this is articulated with their memories of Palestine which they transmit to the new generation born outside Palestine. Mothers and grandmothers do most of this. Women relate narratives of life in Palestine, giving beautiful and romanticized descriptions of social life and relationships in home villages and compare it to the misery of their present daily life. The young people who have never been there repeat the same stories about their former villages; "misfortunes and poverty were explained to children by their parents as a consequence of the loss of homeland" (Peteet 1989:26). The children respond by blaming their parents for leaving their homes, and insist that they should have remained and defended their land instead of fleeing to these "bad places."

Self Representation Pre- and Post Al-Nakba

Palestinian identity has been politicized in the face of constant denial and dispossession in diaspora. Generally speaking, the refugees fall back on their past to overcome their demeaning present. Palestinian refugees in Wadi al-Rimam use two kinds of symbols to show their Palestinian identity, one of them symbolizing their past before 1948, the other invented and reproduced in exile. The selection of these symbols – whether the people are aware of this or not – usually respond to other existing identities. On one hand is the enforcement of the Israeli state, with its continuous efforts to destroy the Palestinian identity, and on the other the different policies of the host countries – in this case Jordan – either to assimilate the Palestinians completely, or to marginalize them. Palestinian refugees find symbols and icons to continue distinguishing themselves from others.

Self Representation as Peasants

Palestinian refugees in Wadi al-Rimam emphasize their peasant origin to demonstrate that they do not belong to their contemporary urban setting. Although "physically" living in a completely urban context, they articulate images and thoughts of being peasants from specific villages in Palestine in their everyday practices in a completely urban context. For example, they use the term *fallah* (peasant) to distinguish themselves from other people in Amman (Jordanians and non-peasant Palestinians). Despite their peasant origin, their current activities use none of their skills as peasants. The majority are working as daily wage labourers on an irregular bases, in construction, in car maintenance, etc. "The *fallah* has been made the symbolic representative of the cultural and historical continuity of the Palestinians. The peasant additionally signifies a prolonged attachment and deep love for the land of Palestine in the face of land expropriations and population transfers by the Israelis" (Swedenberg 1990:168).

The peasant identity is reinforced by the emphasis on speaking the Palestinian peasant dialect. Members of the community are quick to criticize those who mix their Palestinian peasant dialect with other words from Jordanian or urban Palestinian dialects. Women and children who spend most of their time in the valley speak the peasant's dialect more or less unalloyed. Boys and girls from the community who attend UNRWA schools until the ninth grade continue to speak the same peasant Palestinian dialect. These completely free schools are only for Palestinians and most of the teachers are also Palestinian refugees. When the students move to the secondary governmental schools with other students from different backgrounds, the boys start to mix their peasant dialect with the Jordanian dialect while the girls adapt terms from the urban Palestinian dialect. But both boys and girls speak only the peasant Palestinian dialect when they go back to their homes and their community in Wadi al-Rimam.

Another symbol Palestinians reproduce in their daily life is eating habits from the earlier peasant life. For example, olive oil and wild thyme are Palestinian food and powerful symbols of Palestine. The beauty of olive trees and the smell of thyme are now included in many of the songs the women sing while doing housework or in social gatherings. Both men and women tell stories of collecting the wild *zatar* from the fields in the earlier days. They also compare the vegetables and fruits they now buy from Amman with those their fields produced before 1948. Their products were "real" and authentic with a beautiful smell and taste, unlike today's market vegetables which taste like plastic. People in Wadi al-Rimam also emphasize their peasant's identity through dietary practices like eating olives and uncooked onions with all meals. They reminisce of the earlier days when they did not need to spend money on food, since they could eat from their own fields: we had "wheat for bread which we could eat with oil and olives and vegetables in all seasons. If we did not have money, we would not go hungry."

The women spend part of their time every day doing Palestinian embroidery. Younger girls are also encouraged to learn it. Women over the age of forty-five still regularly wear the Palestinian peasant dress (*thawb fallahi*). If a woman from the community goes outside her house without wearing this Palestinian dress, other women will accuse her of trying to be *madaneyya* (urbanized), which is a negative indication that she wants to change her identity and, implicitly, gives up her right to go back to Palestine.

Self Presentation as Refugees

At first, Palestinians considered it to be humiliating to be labelled as refugees. For the Palestinians, it meant a state of inferiority and need. But time has transformed this word, bringing it new meanings and making it more acceptable. Being a refugee has become an identity. A Palestinian from Wadi al-Rimam noted "now, we can't live without this word (refugee), it is a way of showing that we still have a homeland, and we are Palestinians living in temporary exile." In an interview conducted by Salman Rushdie, Edward Said stated "Palestinians are a people who move a lot, who are always carrying bags from one place to another. This gives us a further sense of identity as a people" (Rushdie 1991:174). An older man from Wadi al-Rimam described this refugee identity:

> When we first came to Jordan we hated to be referred to as refugees. This was disgracing and humiliating; it meant that we are poor, waiting for aid from the relief agencies, and no one believed that we [once] had land and big beautiful houses. But now we are proud that we are refugees, and we will stay as refugees until we return to our homes. My refugee card and not my Jordanian passport proves my Palestinian *asil* (origin). Although the name of *Falasteen* (Palestine)

has been changed, my village was demolished and given a Hebrew name, the day will come when all Palestinian refugees and all of their descendent will return home and build Palestine as we built all the Arab countries.

After 1948, UNRWA issued refugee cards for Palestinian refugees to receive aid and UN services. Now although many of these services do not exist any more, almost all refugees have kept their cards and they apply for refugee cards for their newborn children. Not only have needy Palestinians in camps demanded identity cards from UNRWA, but also some wealthier people have argued that refugee cards should be issued to all refugees regardless of their need for relief. The refugee card is a signifier of a temporary, unique status, and a tangible representation of the UN commitment to effect their return to Palestine. "The UNRWA identity cards were like the 'promissory note' on their right to return to Palestine"(Plascov 1981:49).

Conclusion

For a displaced community, narrating the past is often an oppositional process which takes place in the context of political contention and struggle. This process is further animated by the way the identity of the community is constructed by "others," in this case Arabs of the host countries and the Israelis. In the specific case of Wadi al-Rimam, one might say that the existence of thousands of refugees who share similar experiences and construct analogous pasts becomes an "authority" and "power" against all other forces threatening Palestinian identity by creating an obligation on this refugee community to keep and reproduce those practices and customs which have come to constitute the Palestinian "tradition."

References

Bisharat, George
    1994   Displacement and Social Identity: Palestinian Refugees of the West Bank. *In* Population Displacement and Resettlement: Development and Conflict in the Middle East. Ed. by Seteney Shami. New York: Center for Migration Studies.

Khalidi, W.
    1992   All that Remains: The Palestinian Village Occupied and Depopulated by Israel in 1948. Washington D.C.: Institute of Palestine Studies.

Morris, M.
    1986   The Harvest of 1948 and the Creation of the Palestinian Refugee Problem. The Middle East Journal 40(40):671-685.

Peteet, Julie
    1991   Gender In Crisis: Women and the Palestinian Resistance Movement. New York: Columbia University Press.

Plascov, A.
    1981   The Palestinian Refugees in Jordan 1948-1957. London: Frank Press.

Rushdie, Salman
    1991   Imaginary Homelands: Essays and Criticism 1981-1991. London: Penguin Books.

Said, Edward
    1983   A Profile of the Palestinian People. Chicago: Palestine Human Rights Campaign.
    1986   After the Last Sky: Palestinian Lives. New York: Pantheon.

Sayigh, Rosemary
    1977   The Palestinian Identity Among Camp Residents. Journal of Palestine Studies 6(3):3-22.
    1979   Palestinians: From Peasants to Revolutionaries. London: Zed Press.

Swedenberg, Ted
    1990   The Palestinian Peasant As National Signifier. Anthropological Quarterly 63(1).

"Your Papers or Your Life"

The Significance of Documents in the Life Experiences of African Refugees in Israel

Hadas Yaron

Introduction

In the first chapter of *Talks of Refugees* written by Bertolt Brecht a character named "dumpy" shares with its friend named "the big" the following observation:

> The passport is the person's most precious organ. The passport is not made in a simple way as the person does. A person could be created everywhere and in the hastiest manner and with no reason – but the passport shall never. This is why the passport is accepted when it is a good one – while the person could be excellent and still not accepted. [Brecht 1996:7-8]

This statement, as with many others in the book, describes the pain and absurdity in the life experiences of refugees in Europe during the Second World War. Having no "good" document, according to Brecht, supercedes the person, as without the right passport, one is condemned to be "handicapped." In this article I wish on the one hand to draw on Brecht's observation as to the existential importance of the passport in the life experiences of refugees, while I also wish to develop this observation further and point to the complex relationships between persons, identification (ID) papers and other documents throughout people's lives as refugees. In the article I focus on the life events of African refugees living in Israel and the way they perceive and act with their different documents, on their way to Israel and in their lives in the country.

African refugees started to reach Israel through the southern border with Egypt in large numbers in 2006. At the beginning most of the refugees were Sudanese including refugees from southern Sudan and Darfur, and later also large numbers of Eritreans crossed the border and entered the country. The first wave of refugees were people who had lived in Egypt for quite some time, but in the wake of a violent demonstration in front of the United Nations High Commissioner for Refugees (UNHCR) offices in Cairo, the arrests and the other difficulties which featured in their lives in Egypt, made them decide to "take their chances" and cross the border into Israel. Later, African refugees started to travel to Israel from other countries, and some had even planned to reach Israel before they left their home country.

While a few scholars have explored what is defined as "migrant workers" in Israel emphasizing the labour perspective (see Sabar 2008; Kemp and Raijman 2008; Rosenhek 2000; Willen 2003), dealing with either legal workers mostly from Asian countries, or illegal – mostly from Africa, little research has been conducted on African arrivals as refugees and particularly on the wave of thousands of arrivals from Sudan and Eritrea. Therefore while previous research emphasized the absence of documentation, or the documentation of foreign workers, this research wishes to examine the documentation of Africans in Israel as refugees, exploring their ID documents but not from the perspective of employment.

The number of refugees living in Israel is constantly changing and can only be approximately estimated by human rights organizations. Currently, there are about 17,000 African refugees living in the country. Only a much lower number of refugees from Asian and other countries are claiming asylum in Israel. Many of the African refugees are living and working in various cities in the country such as Ashdod, Eilat and Arad, others are held in prisons mainly located in close proximity to the border, while others are spread in various locations such as shelters and agricultural settlements. African refugees are normally imprisoned upon their entry to Israel. According to the authorities, their detention is aimed at identity verification, thus the need for documentation, medical examinations and providing vaccinations. Other refugees are held in prison for violating their "conditions for release." Since the current status of Eritrean and Sudanese refugees is defined as a conditional release and their stay in Israel is geographically defined to allowed and forbidden zones, a violation of their conditions may lead to arrest. In general, the legal status of refugees staying in Israel is complicated and highly dynamic, or as many of the NGOs involved would say "chaotic," as although Israel signed the refugee convention there is no relevant domestic legislation and decisive policy. The State of Israel until recently had no solid asylum system and instead all of the relevant procedures were handled primarily by the UNHCR and approved by the State only at the very last stage of the application. As a result, the UNHCR in Israel plays a crucial role in the lives of refugees. Nevertheless, throughout the years Israel granted asylum through this procedure only to 170 refugees. On the other hand, in the absence of a local refugees' law, the State acts on the basis of local legislation with regards to entering the country instead of international conventions. In the eyes of many of the NGOs the State's policy is to have no policy at all, thereby putting most of the humanitarian weight in providing the needs of the refugees on voluntary shoulders. The attitudes of the government and public towards the African newcomers are complicated and are motivated by fears and indifference as well as compassion, and a sense of special moral obligation as the Jewish nation. The most telling example in this context is the reaction towards the arrival of refugees from Darfur. In Israeli public discourse, refugees from Darfur are often compared to Holocaust survivors.

The comparison between Jewish persecution and African genocide is not reserved for individuals or NGOs but was in fact primarily the reason why a couple of hundred Darfurian refugees were granted residency by the Israeli Government shortly after their arrival in the country in 2007. In certain cases, this approach also expands to refugees from other African countries. One of the reserve soldiers I interviewed, for example, told me that the journey of African refugees from Egypt into Israel reminded him of the borders his family had to cross illegally in Europe. On the other hand, Government officials in public and also private meetings refer to the African refugees coming from Egypt as "infiltrators." The term "infiltrators" not only does not recognize the refugees' need for asylum, but compares them to Palestinian individuals who attempted to enter Israel after the establishment of the Israeli State, and were treated as hostile and dangerous. Therefore while asylum seekers in Israel are associated with Palestinians in the terminology and certain laws enacted in their case, their system of documentation and "processing" is separate and different. One should note that the perception of Africans as hostile unfortunately is also apparent among certain citizens. A recent TV show which used a hidden camera followed a refugee from Congo in the streets of Tel Aviv. Certain people not only showed little empathy towards the refugee but one woman even called the police to arrest him since, as she said, it is a "Jewish State."

I started conducting this research in the summer of 2007 as part of my involvement in an international human rights organization located in Tel Aviv, and later on with other local NGOs. Most of the organizations involved in campaigning and advocating for the refugees are local human rights NGOs such as the "Hotline."[1]

---

1   Please see their website: http://www.hotline.org.il.

Other organizations involved such as the Kibbutz Movement are operating on a humanitarian basis rather than out of a human rights agenda. As a result, the approach of human rights organizations is a more critical one, focusing on changing policy and providing legal aid rather than humanitarian care. And although cooperation and coordination is understood to be crucial by the different parties involved, disagreements and competition is often the practice. In this context, my research is an activist one as I am strongly involved and identify with the activities of certain human rights NGOs. As part of my involvement I collect information, write documents and also assist in the immediate needs of the refugees. This choice of position allows me to deepen my research on the one hand, crossing boundaries and being an active part of the reality I investigate, as much as it narrows prospective exploratory avenues on the other. The material I collect through the different activities such as meetings and demonstrations includes information on the Jewish-Israeli and the African side of the matter, the position of NGOs, the State and the public or society as well as the stories and experiences of refugees. One of the important issues, so I have gathered, which concerns policy and the everyday life of the refugees, is their documentation, the type of documents they carry, and the specifics detailed in or the content of the documents.

In the absence of legislation and related policies, the types of documents the refugees are provided with vary and change with the ongoing changes in policy. Documents refugees possess include passports, national ID cards, UNHCR cards issued elsewhere, and letters provided by the UNHCR office in Israel, letters provided by the Israeli authorities when released from prison, as well as in certain cases ID cards or letters provided by the Israeli interior office. The different documents determine the refugees' name identity, original citizenship, their legal status in Israel, as well as the period and geographical area in Israel in which they are allowed to be employed. The documents therefore define the refugees' legal ability to move and provide for themselves, while their national identity determines their current status in Israel and, as I will explain later, it also provides, together with the personal identity, the basis for their asylum claim in the future. The documents mediate between the refugees and the authorities – the police who might stop them in the street, as well as their employers when they search for a job. The documents therefore enable and define the refugee's most basic needs and define their status, legal and social identity in the country. However, as I will show, refugees do not remain passive in their relationship with documents, but enact and thus demonstrate what I refer to as their "agency." For example, refugees choose to present to officials the documents which they believe will assist them best in certain situations, or they may destroy documents (passports in particular) which they believe can cause them damage. In the next section I wish to identify some theoretical terms which could be of help in analyzing the relationships between the refugees and the documents they carry.

Documents: Persons, Bodies, Representations

In the quote with which I opened the article Brecht describes the passport as "person for precious organ," hence the passport in certain situations could be part of the person's body. On the other hand Brecht also cynically claims that the passport can "supercede" the person; be more important and valuable than the human being it represents. Yet while the first typifies literary writings, the latter has been investigated in academic scholarship. Scholars who investigate the origins and functions of ID documents claim that documents serve nation-states in surveillance and the "maintenance" of their borders and populations (Scott 1998). According to John Torpey (2000) the invention of the passport in Europe was tied to the facilitation of far reaching mass movement, the creation of capitalist spaces out of local ones and the collapse of the pre-national empires such as the Ottoman Empire. The passport regime was strengthened during the inner wars period, empowering totalitarian regimes in controlling and "imprisoning" their citizens or, in the case of other nation states, in building a "wall of papers" against migrants and refugees. Other scholars wish to shed light on other aspects of documentation. Gaston Gordillo (2006) describes the role of ID papers from the perspective of excluded native groups in Argentina and the effect of the deprivation of papers rather than their production. In the past, Gordillo says, the absence of "passports" made travelling through space a dangerous activity for native people, putting them in the vulnerable position of being "savages" who could easily be assaulted. For this reason, he explains, native groups today almost "venerate" their ID papers as material objects. A recent research of the anthropologist Tobbias Kelly among West Bank Palestinians shows that as much as documents enable movements through space, one's "wrong" documents can impose confinement and closure (see Kelly 2007).

We can see therefore, that papers both enable and disable, and that the absence of papers can free individuals as much as it could be a way of classifying and controlling them. Looking again at Brecht, we can say that papers have the potential to fetishize persons, in being their representation but yet an object superior to them and which could erase them. However, papers could also be objects which encapsulate relations rather than erasing them (Riles 2004), and therefore could also function as body parts which enable our everyday life, as well as enabling us to survive extreme situations.

My focus on documents in this article will consider both of those aspects, namely the fetishism of ID papers as well as ID papers as organs, as part of one's body or as a reflection of it. My focus on the latter derives from the testimonies of the refugees, and their interpretation. Therefore, while my interviewees do not describe ID papers literally as bodily organs, I found they made such parallels in speech or practice such as in holding documents close to their bodies and in handing them to me upon meeting them in order to explain who they are, both in their own eyes and in the eyes of the State.

Documents on the Way to, and Throughout the Life in Israel

One cannot underestimate the importance of ID documents on the journey to and in the stay of African refugees in Israel. From the encounters I had and the interviews I have conducted with refugees I found that refugees carry their documents on their bodies almost at all times. In fact, when it comes to objects from their home countries, documents are almost the only objects which they have left as the most precious ones. In most cases refugees are "stripped" of their belongings throughout their travel to Israel by the smugglers and the police in Sudan and Egypt, and also they lose many of the things they brought with them because of the hardship of their journey. One of the soldiers I interviewed, for example, told me that he remembered a photo album probably belonging to one of the refugees who crossed into Israel which was for some reason left and "wandered" around the military post and was later thrown away. Another reserve soldier told me that one night he found refugees' belongings which were caught by the fence in the haste and panic of crossing over and which he collected and gave back to them. Yet in the first encounter with the Israeli military, refugees are requested to present their passports or other ID papers if they have them. And therefore while some of the other objects are replaceable, documents are not necessarily so, and while many of the objects encapsulate the past, documents are the foundation for their future. This is another reason for their special importance, and for that reason documents are guarded close to one's body, often surviving the hardship of the journey.

In certain cases ID documents could also be perceived as the full reflection of a person. For example, one of the activists told me about a young African who was shot by the Egyptian military and died on the Israeli side of the border and was buried as "anonymous" in a Kibbutz. His mother who is in Israel found it hard to accept that it was her son beyond any doubt buried in the Kibbutz, and said that she wanted to see the papers, which would convince her. Although she had not seen her son's body before burial, she did not request its exhumation to verify his death, but instead the ID papers he carried on his body were as evident for her as the body itself. As we shall see, the connection between body and documents has been elaborated also by the authorities in a more scientific vein through the implementation of biometric registration for all refugees.[2] However, while for the authorities the biometric examination aims at (as is also the case nowadays for example at American airports) directly registering one's bodily details, thus overcoming the power of paper documents, for this grieving mother, the documents were the proof for her son's body. Documentation, as these practices show is closely associated with the bodies of persons who escape across borders, and are subjected to anonymous, violent death. Marginality, therefore as I mentioned earlier, emphasizes the fetishizing relationships between persons and their ID documents.

While documents in the tragic case mentioned above define the end of life and the end of one's journey in an attempt to find asylum, for those who manage to cross safely into Israel, ID documents, as I have said, are the basis for their new life in the country. One's citizenship is of particular importance in Israel since in the absence of an individual-based procedure, asylum claimants have been given protection on a collective basis. As a result certain nationalities are more privileged than others. The Darfurians in this context are in the best position in comparison to others. As the survivors of a genocide the public and government are most sympathetic to this community as I have mentioned, and therefore a group of a couple of hundred Darfurians received Israeli residency cards. The documents the refugees carry with them as their passports, the ones they present to the authorities, are the basis for the type of papers they could be given afterwards.

The type of documents the refugees hold and the details specified in them have a strong effect on the way they can manage their lives in the new country. The Israeli documents normally state that the person is permitted to live in certain areas of the country – up north and down south. Therefore the documents define their movement and confine them to certain geographical areas. If they are found elsewhere by the police they could be arrested. In addition, the permit the refugees are given is limited in time, and if refugees are for some reason unable to renew their visas they can easily lose their jobs. The type of documents and the details included such as a photograph could also have a crucial effect. For example, one of the refugees I am in

---

2   The Israeli authorities execute a biometric registration for all asylum seekers which includes for example their fingerprints in order to be able to identify people according to their bodily features and not only by their documents. The asylum seekers receive a document from the police stating they were biometrically registered.

close touch with told me he has been unable to open a bank account for a very long time because he does not have a passport, although he has other documents. Not having an account puts his job in jeopardy and makes him an easy target for robbers because of the large amounts of cash he has to carry on his body. This has been one of the major concerns for this particular young man. Not being able to open a bank account with the papers he is provided often frustrates him. Once while he had a job in Eilat he almost lost his position as the hotel he worked for agreed to pay his salary only through an account, and on another occasion as his room was broken into, he became more anxious about how to protect his money. Yet although documents produced in Israel have a strong effect on the refugees' everyday lives, often as African refugees don't read Hebrew they cannot tell what their content is and what could be their possible effect. One of the refugees told us in an interview that he was brought to the police and then released once he showed his papers, but he cannot tell what is in them, although the papers got him free. Thus, while documents could have such crucial impact affecting one's freedom and preventing deportation, they are illegible to the one who holds them.

Papers enable the State to monitor the presence of African newcomers as much as they facilitate or obstruct the life of refugees. For this reason the documents could be a target for resistance, for the enactment of one's agency. For example, one of the young men I came across who originates from south Sudan lost his papers and then his job and later drastically deteriorated into alcohol and other troubles. His arrests were uncommon incidents since his arrival in the country with his family, after living for many years in Egypt. One of the activists who has been in close touch with this young man suggested that it is possible that the loss of documents was not accidental and was this man's way of "rebelling," acting against the restrictions in having no papers at all. Because he lost his papers he had to travel to Tel Aviv in order to try and procure new papers, and could not continue anymore in the odd job he had in Eilat. The loss of papers provided him with a reason to get away and once more fall into the habit of drinking and sleeping outdoors. I believe that in a way, the loss of papers even if unconsciously and in a destructive manner, was this young man's way of enacting his agency to get away from the life which uprooting and seeking asylum offered him. Similarly, in a few cases I have come across, the destruction of national ID papers and passports by refugees who believe their papers could be harmful to them is a way of attempting to overcome the "wall of papers" and to improve their chances beyond borders. Similarly, one of the refugees from Eritrea told me that in Sudan he had no document provided by the government and felt safer than in

Israel. Thus, for him, the documentation in Israel is a way for the State to control him rather than a way to guarantee his status and safety.

Nevertheless, I have found that, although documents are tools which facilitate the present and hopefully the future they have an emotional aspect which in some cases can supercede pragmatism. One of the refugees I interviewed told me that he had to escape his country under a false name and for security reasons decided not to carry any documents with his original name. Yet, he said it hurts him that he lost his name and cannot be called by it anymore. For him therefore the new passport allowed him to save himself but with it he also lost his past. Other refugees from Ethiopia I was told by one of the members of the community prefer not to declare they are Ethiopians but instead they are Eritreans although the position of the Eritreans in Israel is reasonable because they themselves choose to define themselves as Ethiopians. In these cases, asylum claimants wish the ID documents not only to assist them in finding a new life but to "truly" define who they feel they are. Documents for them are not simply a tool, they are not the State's property but are part of them and therefore should be a faithful reflection of their identity.

Conclusions – Refugees and Dialectics

In this article I have described the complex relationships between persons who are refugees, in this case African refugees, and the documents they carry or have issued to them. As I have shown, in a world in which people are compelled to cross national borders in search of a safe haven, there are different papers – national and transnational – through which they manage and which manage their lives. National ID cards and passports "bring to the world" other papers, while all of the different papers continue to play an important role in the refugees' everyday lives. In that respect, power is not located in one document only, but in the dialectic relations between persons and their documents. They learn from their personal happenings about policies, the significance and content of their documents and strive to either fight or adapt to them.

In this vein, I wish to claim that documents could be perceived on the one hand as one's bodily organ, or as one's reflection, as much as they could be perceived as an instrument which erases one's past and enables one's future, a vital but sometimes an illegible object which determines important moments in one's life. Therefore, we should note, that while States attempt to monitor citizens through documentation, people produce and selectively use them, destroy and lose them in an inevitable search for new lives across national borders.

Acknowledgements

I wish to thank Ilan Lonai at Amnesty International the Israel Section who made this research possible. I also wish to thank Alice Nagle and Johnny Bayu at the African Refugees Development Center in Israel for their enormous help and support in this research.

References

Brecht, Bertolt
   1996 [1961] Talks of Refugees. Tel Aviv: Shoken.

Gordillo, Gaston
   2006   The Crucible of Citizenship: ID-Paper Fetishism in the Argentinean Chaco. American Ethnologist 33(2):163-176.

Kemp Adriana and Rebeca Raijman
   2008   Migrants and Workers: The Political Economy of Labor Migration in Israel. Jerusalem: Van Leer [Hebrew].

Riles, Annelise
   2004   Law as an Object. *In* Law and Empire in the Pacific. S. E. Merry and D. Brenneis, eds. Pp 187-212. Santa Fe: School of American Research Press and James Curry.

Rosenhek, Zeev
   2000   Migration Regimes, Intra State Conflicts and the Politics of Exclusions and Inclusion: Migrant Workers in Israeli Welfare State. Social Problems 47(1):49-67.

Sabar, Galia
   2008   We're Not Here to Stay: African Migrant Workers in Israel and Back in Africa. Tel Aviv: Tel Aviv University Press [Hebrew].

Scott, James C.
   1998   Seeing Like a State: How Certain Schemes to Improve the Human Condition Have Failed. New Haven: Yale University Press.

Torpey, John
   2000   The Invention of the Passport Surveillance Citizenship and the State. Cambridge: Cambridge University Press.

Willen, Sarah S.
   2003   Perspective on Labour Migration in Israel. Revue Europeenne des Migrations Internationales 19:243-262.

A Comment on the Minutemen Militia of the U.S. and Neoliberal State Activity

Devin T. Molina

Introduction

The year 2005 marked a turning point in the immigration debate in the United States. In that year, the Minuteman Project and Civil Homeland Defense joined forces to conduct a month-long border watch near Tombstone Arizona. Since then, Minutemen organizations throughout the United States have continued to participate in border security operations, surveillance efforts at day labour hiring centers, and political protest and advocacy at the municipal, state, and national levels. The Minutemen share their ideological positions on immigration and border security with other anti-immigrant groups. Like other groups, the Minutemen blame immigrants for a variety of social ills, including welfare dependency, deterioration of schools and hospitals, and increased crime. They also fault unprecedented levels of immigration with dramatically altering the political and cultural makeup of the United States. Moreover, they argue that the government is willfully disregarding its duties to protect national sovereignty, secure the borders, and defend U.S. citizens from what they believe is a foreign invasion. They point to neoliberal free trade agreements such as NAFTA and GATT, corporate outsourcing, and corporate demand for cheap and disposable foreign labour as indications of a government that puts foreign and corporate interests before those of its citizens.

At the same time, immigration opponents, as with other members of the Right, have lobbied hard for neoliberal legislation that supports welfare state retrenchment and the end to "Big Government." Promoting neoliberal moralities of personal responsibility, immigration opponents demand punitive solutions to the complex social problems that neoliberalism often fosters, such as permeable borders, social dislocation, heightened social and economic stratification, and the deconstruction of homogenous national groups (Wacquant 2001).

Accordingly, the Minutemen focus their efforts almost exclusively on conducting border security activities. As they observe and report illicit border crossings, the Minutemen are engaged in a dual project. On one hand, the Minutemen seek to exert political pressure on the state to enact harsher border security efforts; on the other, they potentially extend the reach and gaze of the state, thus expanding its ability to exert coercive force on migrants as they cross into the United States (Chavez 2008; Walsh 2008). However, as scholars have noted, the contemporary border security effort is not only largely ineffective, but may be a primarily symbolic effort aimed partly at protecting neoliberal economic aims (Andreas 2001; Cornelius 2001; Massey 2005; Massey and Singer 1995; Purcell and Nevins 2005). In this sense, the Minutemen's insistence on securing the border may in fact only increase the neoliberal effects that they oppose.

In this paper, I analyze Minuteman activity along the U.S.-Mexico border in eastern San Diego County, California. I argue that the Minutemen combine anti-immigrant ideology with border security tactics in ways that challenge *and* support state action. While the Minutemen and the state engage in collaborative efforts, the Minutemen do not effectively broaden the state's ability to successfully stem illicit flows across its borders. Instead, Minuteman activities provide valuable ideological and discursive support to the state that further legitimates failed border security efforts. In addition, because the Minutemen rely exclusively on Border Patrol agents to apprehend and deport undocumented immigrants, the state in turn empowers Minuteman action. Understanding how the Minutemen operate and their relationship to the state can thus provide insight into the relationships between civil society and the state under neoliberalism. Doing so can highlight the ways that neoliberalism remains a dominant yet incomplete process rife with contradictory pressures.

I begin with a brief description of Minuteman ideology and activity, paying close attention to the way that it is both a response to and an outgrowth of neoliberalism. Then I describe two Minuteman "operations" that took place on consecutive weekends in April 2008, arguing that Minuteman and state activity mutually constitute each other in ways that highlight the contradictions inherent in neoliberalism.

The Minutemen as Response to and Outgrowth of Neoliberalism

The emergence of the Minuteman movement can be understood in part as both a product of neoliberalism and a response to the myriad economic, social, and political dislocations that neoliberalism produces. Neoliberalism is a totalizing, though never completed, logic – a political, economic, and ideological process that fuels globalization (Kingfisher 2002; Morgen and Gonzales 2008). Under neoliberal regimes, markets are freed from government regulation and interference, including reduced or eliminated corporate taxation, the protection and expansion of private property rights, and the elimination of barriers to trade. Markets rather than states are believed to best organize economic, political, and social life.

The transformation of the market is thus accompanied by the transformation of the state and society. Welfare spending is reduced while the state trains its focus on securing the rights of capital. The state increasingly relies on the private sector to provide public services such as education, health care, welfare, and policing. Keynesian logics of state activity that once promoted state intervention aimed at protecting citizens from the negative effects of unregulated capitalism are replaced by ideologies of personal responsibility that force the public to absorb the economic and social costs of neoliberalism (Duggan 2003; Giroux 2008).

Between 1986 and 2003 cross border flows between Mexico and the United States increased dramatically with the largest growth occurring after the passage of NAFTA in 1994 (Massey 2005). By 2003 trade between the two countries totalled over \$235 billion. Individuals crossing into the United States for work and vacation numbered in the hundreds of thousands and millions respectively. Total border crossings increased from 114 million in 1986 to over 290 million in 2000 (4-5). At the same time, both documented and undocumented migration steadily continued to rise. Whereas legal immigration averaged 330,000 per year in the 1960s, by the 1990s that number had climbed to over 1 million per year (Massey 1999:316). Similarly, for the period of 1965-1989 undocumented migration grew from only 87,000 per year to between 1.2 and 1.5 million entries per year (Massey and Singer 1995). Today undocumented immigration averages 500,000 entries per year (Passel and Cohn 2008).

According to the Minutemen, when Mexican and Latin American immigrants cross into the United States, they bring with them poverty, crime, a different language, and cultural norms that are fundamentally and drastically different from our own. The introduction of Third World poverty that Mexican and Latin American migrants represent threatens to dramatically alter the cultural, political, and economic fabric of

American life. That many Latin American migrants apparently flaunt the rule of law by crossing into the United States without authorization provides the Minutemen further proof of the threat that unchecked immigration poses: the breakdown of the "rule of law." The Minutemen thus participate in a discursive project that not only positions immigrants outside the bounds of the nation, but also positions them outside the bounds of proper personhood (Kingfisher and Maskovsky 2008). The Minutemen thus lay claim to a neoliberal morality that valourizes their "service" as a volunteer force in defense of the nation against an exterior threat.

Immigrants are not the Minutemen's only or perhaps even the primary target of their vitriolic attacks. By tying undocumented immigration to a neoliberal morality, the Minutemen further demonize those who fail to or refuse to participate in the defense of the homeland. According to the Minutemen, immigrants, their supporters, and an apathetic government are equally to blame for the current immigration "crisis." The Minutemen view U.S. participation in neoliberal free trade economic agreements such as NAFTA and their participation in international organizations such as the World Trade Organization as an abdication of the state's sovereign duty to protect its citizens' interests and its own national and territorial integrity. At best, the state has failed to secure the border; at worst it is deliberately trying to weaken national security in the interests of global capital. The failure of the U.S. government to secure the border thus represents the primary impetus behind Minuteman activity. Filling the gaps left by the state is therefore the primary tactical logic employed by the Minutemen to put pressure on the state to enforce the "rule of law" and to stop the foreign "invasion." In some ways the Minutemen's opposition to the government is a product of neoliberal ideologies, namely that the government is incapable of effectively governing. In other ways the Minutemen oppose what they view as government policies that limit the state's ability to secure the nation from outside threats.

The Minutemen thus argue that unchecked mass migration from Mexico and Latin America poses a serious threat to national security. Whereas typical anti-immigrant calls for the exclusion of Latin American immigrants are based on the perceived economic and cultural impacts that immigration poses, the Minutemen differ by emphasizing border security as the primary method of controlling immigration. For them, terrorism and "illegal" immigration are two sides to the same coin. An insecure border allows terrorist and immigrant alike to challenge the state's ability to protect its borders and thus diminish state sovereignty. Merging conspiracy theories such as the Mexican *reconquista* with nationalistic paranoia, economic alarmism, and white supremacist constructions of the nation, the Minutemen believe that mass migration is therefore not only a drain on the economy and a challenge to the American nation as a white Protestant nation; it is also a direct and immediate threat to national security and national sovereignty. Thus, the Minutemen call for the expansion of state policing activities on the border and an expansion of the punitive capacities of the state vis-à-vis immigrants.

To better illustrate these points, I now turn to a brief description of a series of events that took place over the course of two subsequent weekends at Camp Vigilance, the Minuteman Corps of California's (MCC) headquarters, in April 2008. I focus on how Minuteman definitions of success highlight the way that Minuteman and state activity mutually constitute and legitimate each other in service to the broadening of an already repressive border security regime.

Camp Vigilance

Camp Vigilance is an 8 acre private site located approximately 50 miles east of San Diego and two miles north of the border. Since 2006, members of the Minuteman Corps of California have been "mustering" at Camp Vigilance for one weekend each month and for the entire months of April and October. Camp Vigilance functions as a headquarters for Minuteman border patrol operations. During these operations, armed members, utilizing a variety of surveillance technologies such as binoculars, night vision scopes, and thermal imaging cameras, observe, track, and report unauthorized border crossers to the Border Patrol. Camp Vigilance consists of an office trailer that serves as the communications center (Comm. Center) where a volunteer operates a two-way radio and coordinates each operation relaying observed border incursions to the Border Patrol, and a bunkhouse. There are also a number of RV hookups and ample space for tent camping.

I woke at approximately 4 a.m. to the sound of a Minuteman outside my tent urging me to wake up. A team up at the "Eye in the Sky" – a makeshift Mobile Surveillance Unit (MSU) consisting of a thermal camera mounted atop an SUV and operated via remote from within – had spotted a group of twenty migrants heading towards camp. As they tracked the group through the camera their quarry had disappeared from view as they neared Camp Vigilance. The team at the Eye requested aid in finding the group. I, along with everyone else who was not currently out on ops, was mobilized to go out and find the "illegals."

Upon waking, I headed to the Comm. Center where Carl Braun, head of the MCC at the time, asked if I wanted to join him in the search. I agreed as did a long-time and highly active female volunteer, Tara. Carl drove us south past the Camp

Vigilance entrance. The truck shook violently as we traversed the unpaved and poorly maintained local roads. Carl proceeded with caution, slowly inching his way towards the site where the group of migrants was first spotted. Carl told me that he wanted to head back south of the property so that we could prevent the "illegals" from "TBSing" or turning back south. As we drove, Carl and Tara searched the desert scrub to either side of the road for signs of people hiding. They also looked for trail sign, footprints that they could later use to track their quarry. Tara was using a new night vision scope that she had recently bought for over a thousand dollars. The moonless night and the bouncing truck made it difficult for Tara to see so she periodically told Carl to slow down. Other than that Tara did not say much, preferring instead to let Carl do most of the talking.

When Carl is not busy running the largest Minuteman organization in California, or hunting "bad guys," he is an executive recruiter who specializes in minority hiring. A prolific writer, Carl has self-published two techno-thriller novels about international terrorism and military special operations, a non-fictional account of his experience at the border that chronicles the first two years of the California Minutemen, and a huge body of news reports for Examiner.com. As head of the MCC he has also spent a great deal of time speaking to the media and the public on immigration and border issues. As a result, Carl speaks with an easy, if slightly rehearsed, demeanor. The strength of his convictions comes through not as a passionate appeal to one's emotions, but as a carefully considered and rational appeal to "common sense." Even when Carl would delve into the realm of conspiracy theories about a New World Order that is designing to overthrow U.S. sovereignty in favour of a global state, the cadence of his delivery and the timbre of his voice never changed.

As we drove in search of the group of "illegals," Carl told me that the Minutemen are simply a neighbourhood watch organization. As with any other neighbourhood watch, they are on the lookout for criminals and trespassers. Carl admitted that given the size of the "illegal immigration" problem, looking for twenty illegals would not seem to be worth the trouble. But, he told me, we're not looking for a bunch of "strawberry pickers." According to Carl, twenty percent of "illegals" are deported criminals and statistically speaking, four to five people in this group were probably criminals. To prove his point, Carl told me about a woman who lived in Northern California. Married to a Minuteman who was the head of a Northern California chapter, she was the victim of a hit and run committed by an "illegal" who was driving drunk. The driver smashed into her, pinning her between two cars that severed her legs. This, he said, was indicative of the problem we had: criminal aliens with no respect for the rule of law.

But illegal immigration was just a symptom of a larger problem, he said. Banks and corporations, he said, are in a conspiracy to destroy our economy and move us into a depression so that they can form a North American Union. They are manufacturing a money crisis that will usher in the end of America as a sovereign nation as Mexico, Canada, and the United States become part of one borderless nation. This story was one that many Minuteman members told me. One member insisted to me that the Amero, the North American Union currency, was already being minted. Another told me that there were FEMA refugee camps already being assembled in Texas to deal with the victims of the coming economic crisis.

These two narratives, though less than mainstream, are remarkable not because of their resemblance to fact, but because they reveal how the Minutemen conceptualize the problem of immigration. According to Carl, immigration and criminality are necessarily linked. Images of the hardworking, poorly paid, and highly exploited immigrant labourer merely mask the true dangers of immigration. Moreover, immigration is just part of a broader pattern which includes corporate desires to conduct business freely across international boundaries and free from governmental influence, a sentiment that is shared by individuals across the political spectrum. According to Carl, the failure of the government to secure its borders is a sign that the government has become beholden to corporate interests at the expense of its citizens and its own sovereignty. This, he told me was why we were out at four o'clock in the morning searching the high desert of eastern San Diego County.

As time passed and it became increasingly clear that we would not catch our quarry, Carl and Tara began to lose hope. Carl's mood vacillated between optimism and frustration. He joked, "at least we ruined their day a little." But then his voice took on a hard edge as he defiantly spoke to the night: "You don't belong in my country buddy."

A Border Patrol jeep approached us and stopped next to us. The agent, a young male in his twenties, told us that they had been busy all night. They had already caught three groups of "illegals" in the surrounding area, but were still searching the ones that had passed through Camp Vigilance. He did not seem optimistic that they would be found.

We headed back to camp. As he drove, Carl began to strategize out loud and came up with a plan for the next time groups of immigrants try to cross the border through Camp Vigilance. The plan consisted of trapping the "illegals" on the property by closing off all exits and surrounding them on the property. Without a way to get to their destination or TBS, they would voluntarily sit down when confronted by the Minutemen and wait patiently for the Border Patrol to come and pick them up.

A week later Carl and the rest of the Minutemen got a chance to put their plan into action. A team at the Eye in the Sky spotted two groups of about twenty migrants marching down the same road as the previous weekend's group. This time they tracked the migrants until they reached the MSU at which time they "lit up" the group with their headlights. Startled, the groups scattered in every direction. At this point the entire camp was alerted. Someone rang the dinner bell. Bedlam erupted as individuals sought their firearms, protective clothing, and their vehicles. As they waited at their assigned locations, Carl's voice came through on the radio informing the Camp that they had caught twenty-eight individuals. Within minutes a single Border Patrol agent escorted a man, his hands tied with a plastic zip tie past our position. Less than a minute later, out of the darkness followed a group of fourteen men tied to each other and walking in a line. All told, Border Patrol confirmed that forty-four migrants had been apprehended on or near the Camp Vigilance property. Back at Camp what began as a chaotic morning settled into a calm yet euphoric mood that infected everyone. Each individual told and retold their part in the successful capture of such a large group. Carl and the Eye in the Sky team returned with a video taken from the thermal camera.

According to Carl and the other Minutemen, this operation, unlike the previous weekend, had been a complete success. It remains unknown how many individuals attempted to cross through the property. What the Minutemen did know was that by adopting new tactics they turned what had been an abject failure the week before into a successful effort. They had thus played a primary role in the "capture" of more than forty individuals. To demonstrate their success to others, the Minutemen posted the video onto YouTube and posted details of the night's events on the Minuteman Civil Defense Corps website. The purpose of taking the video and posting the report was to highlight the severity of the "illegal immigration problem," to highlight the Minutemen's apparent success, and to request assistance from other Minuteman volunteers.

The preceding examples suggest that the Minutemen do not determine organizational success solely by their ability to stop "illegal immigration." As with state border surveillance efforts, Minuteman activity is a largely theatrical endeavour that projects an image of both an out of control and a secure border (Andreas 2001). Lacking any institutional structure designed to maintain comprehensive statistics about their impact and recognizing their own tactical limitations, Minuteman activity represents a collection of snapshots that create a collage of collective memories tied to the *legitimacy of border security strategies*. These momentary victories give truth to the lie that "securing the border" is the most effective way to stem "illegal immigration."

The Minutemen further claim success despite having relied on state agents to ultimately carry out the apprehensions. What would have happened if the Border Patrol refused to answer the Minutemen's call? What if, as is often the case, the Border Patrol was not able to apprehend the groups of immigrants that the Minutemen observed? As the above example shows, the Minutemen depend on a responsive state in order to achieve their organizational and political goals. Ultimately, the efficacy of their activity depends in large part on the Border Patrol's willingness and ability to translate observed activity into apprehensions.

Not only could the Minutemen not function without the state, but the Minutemen derive much of their legitimacy from state institutions. State activity provides both the template upon which Minuteman activity is based and the logic which informs its tactics. Minutemen are limited in their capabilities because they lack the authority of the state to apprehend and deport undocumented immigrants. This dependence also creates tensions. Driven by neoliberal logics that value their ability to be "self governing" people "who operate independently of formal state structures" (Hyatt 2001:206), the Minutemen nonetheless require the formal state apparatus designed to apprehend, process, incarcerate, and deport unauthorized border crossers to achieve their organizational and political ends. To do this, the Minutemen take steps to act *like* the state, even if they cannot ever act *as* the state. One way they do this is by adopting tactics that will position themselves in situations that will guarantee apprehensions while avoiding actually arresting individuals (an act that is illegal). It was for this reason that Carl insisted on trapping the groups of migrants on the Camp Vigilance property.

Due to their participation at both organizational and individual levels in broader Right and anti-immigrant networks, the Minutemen can more effectively articulate the dangers of an unsecure border to the public in ways that the Border Patrol cannot. The Minutemen, rather than operating as the state's "eyes and ears" (Walsh 2008), instead act as its voice. In order to act as the state's voice, the Minutemen must insert themselves into classificatory processes that take place at the border. According to Josiah Heyman (1999), border security agents participate in innumerable classificatory interactions daily. Agents enact legal classifications as they make snap decisions about who can and cannot legally enter the United States. These judgments are based in part on covert classificatory systems that judge the "moral worth" of a subject. Knowledge production about the good/bad immigrant takes place through the actions of border security agents and their interactions with border crossers.

In the example I provide, the Minutemen were able to successfully insert themselves into this classificatory process. That the Minutemen limit their action exclusively to border security efforts means that they primarily encounter immigrants that are in the process of or have already broken the law. By focusing on border security – instead of for example worksite enforcement or other forms of surveillance activities – they take much of the guesswork out of classification. *Immigrants are always already criminals.* As part of a broad network of anti-immigrant and conservative organizations, the Minutemen are much better suited than the government to translate those classifications to a broader audience as part of a comprehensive statement about the perils of immigration and the merits of border security efforts.

Conclusion

Whether or not the Minutemen are able to stop the flow of people across the border – they are not – or substantially increase the ability of the Border Patrol to do its job – they do not – is irrelevant when we consider how dominant modes of border security impact their activities. Like the Border Patrol, the Minutemen are engaged in symbolic border policing activities that are nevertheless articulated through the use of force and the threat of force. This complex of interaction legitimates the participation of the Minutemen in border security activities. Interestingly, the closer they come to acting *like* the state the more legitimate and accepted their actions become by the Border Patrol. As their actions become more routine, as they successfully insert themselves into the classificatory system at the border, and as they carry out border security operations that parallel in substance, and on occasion by result, those enacted by official representatives, the Minutemen are able to routinely call on the state agents to enact their anti-immigrant aims. What is more, by participating in similar border security activities to those of state institutions, the Minutemen further legitimize an increasingly powerful security apparatus designed to exert coercive force on marginal populations. Acting as engaged witnesses of daily border crossings, the Minutemen articulate both the immigration problem as well as the need for more security resources at the border. Detailing the interactions between the Minutemen and the Border Patrol reveals the way that already powerful forces of border securitization combine with anti-immigrant ideologies to set the parameters within which the Minutemen operate and how they determine their efficacy. A significant result of this process is the routinization of Minuteman behaviour as an extension of border security operations that further articulates the supremacy of border security as immigration control.

When situated within a political economic analysis, this interaction between state and non-state actors reveals the complex ways that illiberal anti-immigrant ideologies collide and combine with the expansion of the state's policing capabilities to promote and protect neoliberal formations such as permeable borders, the production of proper personhood and state activity, and the production of new markets and the deregulation of old ones (most notably the labour market). This research thus suggests that understanding the Minutemen's dependence on the state might explain how a social movement that at first glance appears to be opposed to (at least some aspects of) neoliberalism and that seeks to mitigate its effects might ostensibly act in ways that actually augment the ability of neoliberalism to further penetrate into the fabric of American life. Understanding how the Minutemen and other reactionary groups like them are engaged in activities that both support and undermine their own political aims highlights some of the contradictions inherent in the neoliberal project.

References

Andreas, Peter
> 2001   Border games : Policing the U.S.-Mexico Divide. Ithaca: Cornell University Press.

Chavez, Leo R.
> 2008   Spectacle in the Desert: The Minuteman Project on the U.S.-Mexico Border. *In* Global Vigilantes: Anthropological Perspectives on Justice and Violence. D. Pratten and A. Sen, eds. Pp. 25-46. New York: Columbia University Press.

Cornelius, Wayne a
> 2001   Death at the Border: Efficacy and Unintended Consequences of US Immigration Control Policy. Population and Development Review 27(4):661-685.

Duggan, Lisa
> 2003   The Twilight of Equality: Neoliberalism, Cultural Politics, and the Attack on Democracy. Boston: Beacon Press.

Giroux, Henry A.
> 2008   Against the Terror of Neoliberalism : Politics Beyond the Age of Greed. Boulder, CO: Paradigm Publishers.

Heyman, Josiah McC.
  1999   United States Surveillance Over Mexican Lives at the Border: Snapshots of an Emerging Regime. Human Organization 58(4):430-438.
Hyatt, Susan Brin
  2001   From Citizen to Volunteer: Neoliberal Governance and the Erasure of Poverty. *In* The New Poverty Studies: The Ethnography of Power, Politics, and Impoverishmed People in the United States. J. Goode and J. Maskovsky, eds. Pp. 201-235. New York: New York University Press.
Kingfisher, Catherine
  2002   Introduction: The Global Feminization of Poverty. *In* Western Welfare in Decline: Globalization and Women's Poverty. C. Kingfisher, ed. Pp. 3-12. Philadelphia: University of Pennsylvania Press.
Kingfisher, Catherine, and Jeff Maskovsky
  2008   Introduction: The Limits of Neoliberalism. Critique of Anthropology 28(2):115-126.
Massey, Douglas S.
  1999   International Migration at the Dawn of the Twenty-First Century: The Role of the State. Population and Development Review 25(2):303-322.
  2005   Backfire at the Border: Why Enforcement without Legalization Cannot Stop Illegal Immigration. Cato Institute Trade Policy Analysis (29):1-14.
Massey, Douglas S., and Audrey Singer
  1995   New Estimates of Undocumented Mexican Migration and the Probability of Apprehension. Demography 32(2):203-203.
Morgen, Sandra, and Lisa Gonzales
  2008   The Neoliberal American Dream as Daydream: Counter-hegemonic Perspective on Welfare Restructuring in the United States. Critique of Anthropology 28(2):219-236.
Passel, Jeffrey S., and D'Vera Cohn
  2008   Trends in Unauthorized Immigration: Undocumented Inflow Now Trails Legal Inflow. Washington, D.C.: Pew Hispanic Center.
Purcell, Mark, and Joseph Nevins
  2005   Pushing the Boundary: State Restructuring, State Theory, and the Case of U.S.-Mexico Border Enforcement in the 1900s. Political Geography 24:211-235.
Wacquant, Loïc
  2001   The Advent of the Penal State is not a Destiny. Social Justice 28(3):81-87.
Walsh, James
  2008   Community, Surveillance and Border Control: the Case of the Minuteman Project. *In* Surveillance and Governance: Crime Control and Beyond. M. Deflem, ed. Sociology of Crime, Law and Deviance. Bingley, UK: Emerald.

RACISM AS A TRANSNATIONAL PROCESS
Afro-Cubans Between the Sword and the Wall[1]

Anthony Marcus

This family was upper middle class before the revolution. They never lost their house to the revolution. They aren't that different from my own family. They understand what Americans are used to and they can provide it mostly. They understand us – they have relatives in Miami. The daughter even knows English. It's nicer than staying in some little apartment in old Havana, where the walls are falling down and the only foreign language they know is Russian.

Henry, an American journalist in Havana, 1995

Introduction

So spoke an American freelance journalist who was researching a story on Cuba as it changes from communism to capitalism. While in Havana he was paying $20 per night to stay at a *casa privada* run by a relatively comfortable white Cuban family, who live in an attractive well kept town house in the quiet and airy Havana neighbourhood of Vedado. *Casas privadas* are private houses where families rent out rooms and provide meals to foreign visitors in exchange for dollars to purchase things that they no longer receive from the government. All over Cuba *casas privadas* compete for the foreigner's $20 per night – which is about 2-3 times the average monthly wage of a doctor or engineer working for the government.

1   I received funding for research from CUNY Caribbean exchange. I wish to thank Mary Lemon for her invaluable contributions to my ethnography; Robert Marcus for convincing me to write the paper and then being there with his editor's pen when it was finished; Marc Edelman for helping me to clarify my thinking on Cuba; Tracy Morgan and Michael Weinstein for boundless support and thoughtful discussions; Molly Doane, Charles Menzies, Jonathan Heam, Eliza Darling, and the 15 de Marzo group for useful editorial commentary; Philippe Bourgois, whose book *Ethnicity at Work* did much to shape my thinking about race in the Americas; and Martha Rodriguez who enables New York City and Cuba to share ideas and cultures.

In expressing his preference for staying with a family that was middle class before the revolution and still lives in its old town house in Vedado, this American journalist unconsciously became part of a much larger transnational process of racial inequality that threatens the gains made by Afro-Cubans in the Cuban revolution. This journalist, who regards himself as a very liberal and non-racist American, is open-minded enough to travel to Cuba, in violation of U.S. travel restrictions. However, it never occurred to him that racial divisions had anything to do with him staying with "a middle-class family" that has relatives in the United States rather than a less cultured and cosmopolitan family that lives in a crowded urban neighborhood like Old Havana. He was doing what any of us – other than an anthropologist – would do: using his $20 per night to stay at the most comfortable and familiar place he could find.

Instead of staying with an Afro-Cuban family in Old Havana, an historically Afro-Cuban neighborhood that is falling apart as the Cuban revolution crumbles, he was staying in a house with people who regularly receive money from their relatives in Miami to pay for paint, plaster, and other basic commodities that have lately become unavailable in Cuba. The daughter has learned some English instead of the Russian that was taught in the Cuban schools until recently, because of contact with cousins who live in the United States. While he stays with them, Henry will probably have his clothing cleaned by a relative of the family; he will use taxis called by the family; and he will occasionally use the daughter as an interpreter during interviews. But as the Miami Cubans continue to help out their families on the island with regular cheques, the number of Henrys increases, and the Cuban government continues to struggle against brutal shortages in the state sector, the equality that the Cuban revolution has boasted of for 35 years will continue to erode and differentiation will occur.

These dollars from outside the island as they interact with life in Cuba cause big changes and re-create the very way Cubans see themselves and their neighbours. This paper explores the new dangers and new opportunities in the increasingly interconnected and interdependent economic and political system of the Americas. In particular it examines some of the ways in which the introduction of an internal market economy and the opening of Cuba to the economy and society of the capitalist world has differently affected the lives and perceptions of Afro-Cuban and their non-African identified compatriots.

Racism Transnationally

As with the Jews before them who seemed to be hated by a multitude of peoples in a multitude of different countries in rather similar ways, peoples of the African diaspora have often heard the cross-cultural query, "if blacks are really the same as whites, why is it that they are always at the bottom of every society?" While there are some interesting examples of countries and regions where this is not the case such as Panama, where Afro-Panamanians have been considered to be middle class throughout much of the twentieth century, blacks provide an often sizable and socially very visible component of the poorest and most embattled sectors of society in much of the Americas.

Stereotyped in literature, popular culture, and mass media as a kind of perpetual urban problem, negative images of black people are present even in places where there are no significant African descended populations. In Asia, where there are virtually no black people, the prime minister of Japan provoked a scandal by making racist comments about black people and "Darky Toothpaste," a brand of toothpaste showing an offensively stereotypical African-American minstrel player with bright white teeth and a top hat, has been widely marketed. The drama of American race relations plays out on a world stage with those of African descent representing an international symbol of backwardness and social dysfunction.

While various forms of racism and tribalism have existed since ancient times, the anti-black racism of the present United States represents a more sharply defined and globally uniform racism than its older counterparts. In the pre-capitalist world, racism tended to be a more local set of prejudices based on a variety of characteristics that could be as particular as what kind of clothes people wore, what language they spoke, what god they prayed to, what kind of food they ate, or what specific country or region they came from. As capitalism brought the whole world together into one global system in the eighteenth and nineteenth centuries, whole sections of humanity were grouped into categories described as scientific but actually founded on biologically meaningless sets of superficial physical traits such as skin colour, hair texture, or the dimensions of the head. Racism became even more globally uniform during World War II and through the entire postwar period, when the United States became the most powerful country in the world. Its economic structures, armies, products, television, radio, and media culture, military bases and its "American Dream" spread to the far corners of the globe. Not surprisingly, many of the U.S. understandings of race and racism accompanied these other aspects of American culture.

The process continues into the present with the increased globalization of the U.S. economy, the collapse of the Soviet Union as a counterweight to U.S. influence in Latin America and around the globe, and the widespread introduction of satellite broadcasts of U.S. cable television throughout the Americas. There is hardly a spot in the Americas where one can't watch Baywatch. With the full hemispheric economic integration that is planned for the year 2005, constantly improving communications technology, the increasing domination on a day-to-day basis of the United States and U.S. ideas, the transnationalization of racism, racial political economy, and racial ideologies in the Americas and beyond is very likely to increase.

While large sections of Latin America trace their ancestry back to Africa and Africans, many writers and social scientists have observed that most of the Spanish-speaking countries draw much less of a line between black and white than occurs in the United States. Seeing race more in terms of culture than biology, Latin Americans believe much less that "one drop of black blood" makes someone black. With many, sometimes hundreds of different categories, terms, and nicknames for describing a wide variety of peoples with a wide variety of combinations of colours, features, and social classes there is generally less of a sense that "racial difference" is a fundamental divide. The old saying in Spanish that "money whitens" suggests the ways in which race does influence social standing, but it is more "flexible" and "permeable" than in the United States.

This is not to say that racism against African descended people does not exist in Latin America. It is clear from looking at any set of economic statistics or doing interviews with a wide variety of different people that "blackness" is generally a social disadvantage in Latin America and whiteness an advantage. However, those who consider themselves to be Afro-Latin and are regarded as black are often part of specific communities that are only a small percentage of the people who have some African ancestry.

Cuba, a small island nation, ninety miles off the coast of Florida, has a history of race relations in many ways more like that of the United States than Latin America. The second to last country in the Americas to abolish slavery in 1886, Cuba has a long history of racial segregation, laws against intermarriage between black and white, separate cultural identifications for black and white, and a history of lynchings culminating in the "little war of 1912," an episode of mass lynching and torture of Afro-Cubans, in response to a struggle for civil rights.

Like much of the Caribbean, Cuba saw a retreat of European influence and a rise of U.S. domination in the last decades of the nineteenth century. The central prize that the U.S. fought over in the Spanish-American War, Cuba is both the largest island in the Caribbean and the closest one to the United States (90 miles from Florida). It has for over a century been considered a crucial part of U.S. "hemispheric defense" and was briefly considered for statehood after the war with Spain. Cuba was occupied by the U.S. military in 1898-1901, 1906-1909, 1912, and again in 1917. From the American warships dispatched to the island by Franklin Delano Roosevelt in 1933, in response to the political reformist regime led by Dr. Ramon Grau San Martin to the U.S.-led invasion of the Bay of Pigs in 1961 there has been a long history of U.S. intervention into the internal affairs of Cuba. A U.S. military force remains to this day at Guantanamo Bay on the far eastern end of the island. Throughout much of the twentieth century, this direct U.S. control of Cuba was combined with a tremendous financial and institutional influence of U.S. corporations and organized crime leading pre-revolutionary Cuba to have many of the appearances of a U.S. colony.

This "intimate" relationship between Cuba and the United States during much of the twentieth century may have further added to the similarities between racial divisions in the U.S. and Cuba, doing much to create a separate group that identifies as black. Cuba, though, unlike the rest of the Caribbean and Latin America, had a radical rupture with the economic, political, and social system of the Americas. In 1959, when the July 26th movement seized power in Cuba and installed Fidel Castro as the leader of the government, Cuba began a social trajectory that linked it to a different world system than that of the capitalist countries of the Americas. On April 16, 1961, the night before the Bay of Pigs invasion, when Castro gave a speech at the funeral for victims of a U.S. bombing attack declaring that henceforth the Cuban revolution would be a socialist revolution, he embarked on a development path that brought Cuba closer to the workers' states of eastern Europe.

Even before this breach with the United States, Castro officially addressed the problem of racism in Cuban life. In one of his first speeches as leader of Cuba in March 1959 he shattered the long-standing taboo against even admitting to the existence of racism in Cuba. In this speech he asserted that "one of the battles which we must prioritize ... is the battle to end racial discrimination." Cuba embarked on a radical course including literacy programs and affirmative action for all disadvantaged sectors without regard to colour or background, with the goal of completely integrating all social groups into every aspect of the collective economy and the ending of segregation. While many scholars have assessed the success of these programs and many documented studies suggest that "pre-revolutionary" racial attitudes persist among many white Cubans (Serviat 1986; Carneado 1962; Moore 1988; Casal 1979), there is little doubt that for black Cubans these developments represented an unprecedented increase in relative social power.

The private school system which had formerly been the reserve of whites was eliminated and replaced with an integrated free public school system. Rents were dramatically lowered, with many houses simply deeded over to the inhabitants, (currently eleven years of residence constitutes automatic ownership of a house), making black Cubans the African descended population with by far the highest house ownership percentage in the world. With guarantees of adequate food, health care, housing, education, equal opportunity in employment, and a job for everyone, economically the revolution represented a major improvement in living conditions for all those at the bottom of the social opportunity structure, many of whom were Afro-Cubans. Post revolutionary Cuba has clearly been the country with the least inequality between blacks and whites in the Americas.

Race and Racism in Revolutionary Cuba

A significant percentage of the Cuban population identifies itself with Africa, "black-ness," and the history of slavery in Cuba. One Afro-Cuban put it, "we are different. I knew people in my family who were born slaves. That is why we Cubans went to Africa (the Angola Campaign and the Ethiopian intervention) to help free our brothers who are still enslaved. We have special feelings about Africans." Another black Cuban described her emotions about her daughter having married a white man: "It was difficult at first, because we had to get used to him. At first I didn't want my daughter to marry a white. We black Cubans see whites as less attractive, the whites do not know our culture and there are many compromises that are necessary." Statements like these and the frequent references to the recent history of slavery as an historical experience reveal a consciousness of being both Cuban and yet different from other Cubans.[2]

White Cubans are sharply aware of blackness and Africaness as a social differ-ence. They retain many stereotypical notions of black Cubans that are considered "pre-revolutionary." During an evening music and dance program on Cuban tele-vision the white Cubans with whom I was watching the show made numerous

---

2   While Afro-Cubans make frequent references to the collective memory of slavery, there was no men-tion of the race war of 1912. This war diminutively called "la guerrita del 12."(the little war of 12) saw the deaths of thousands of blacks and ordinary civilians through direct fighting and brutal torture. Cubans of mixed African/European descent, reputedly the majority of Cuba, seem to have little in the way of a separate racially-based cultural identity.

comments about how wonderful black Cubans were at dancing. Recognizing that these comments deviated from a social norm, they expressed defensiveness in the absence of any criticism or questioning on my part. As one woman said, "it isn't racist to say that blacks have something inside them that makes their dancing special. I can say the same thing about Cubans in general. They are better dancers than Americans. This is not racist. Look at them: there is nothing better." Clearly her comments about Afro-Cubans made her defensive in the presence of strangers from the United States.

Some white Cubans were much more explicit about their racialist beliefs. Claiming that communism had ruined Cuba and that the anti-Castro Cubans in the United States "still valued white people," these comments usually accompanied the English word nigger and invectives about Castro's rule. As one self-employed white Cuban told me, "the communist system makes blacks equal, but that is not natural and would be different under capitalism." Such attitudes were rare, and were invariably connected to identification with the United States or Cubans living there. This starkly confirmed the belief among most of my informants that whatever their personal feelings were about black Cubans, "to be a good and patriotic communist" was to reject the racism that they are taught is endemic to capitalism and imperialism. In a society in which the workforce is well integrated, salaries are roughly equal between black and white, and there is little residential or educational segregation, most Cubans appear to be very tolerant of differences or perceived differences.

Because of the great improvements in standards of living and opportunities, Afro-Cubans tend to be among the strongest defenders of Castro and the communist system. One older Afro-Cuban who told me "our memory of slavery is very recent," became nearly enraged when I asked him whether Cuba would ever be led by a black Cuban. "There already are black Cubans who lead this country," he said. "Look at any government office, look at the military, look at the National Assembly you will see all the colours of Cuba. There is not a country in the world that has done more for black people than Cuba. Our infant mortality rates are lower for blacks than the United States, literacy is higher, for blacks than anywhere in the world, our salaries are the same as white people's, nobody keeps us out of their imperialist suburbs, and I don't worry that my son will be beaten to death by a bunch of right-wing racist policemen. There isn't a father any place in the Americas who can say that, except Cubans. Castro is not white he is one of us."

While some Afro-Cubans noted that, indeed, more white Cubans than black ones sat at the very top of the Cuban government, the identification of Castro as "our leader and one of us" was very strong. Several black Cubans were quick to point out that "Castro was a good friend of Malcolm X." While Castro seems to still be very popular generally, Afro-Cubans were far more intensely loyal to "Fidel," the accomplishments of the Cuban revolution, and the communist system that has been in place for about 35 years than most other Cubans, particularly whites. As one Afro-Cuban woman said to me when she told the story of how the Havana town house that she had worked in as a servant before the revolution was given to her when the family that had lived there escaped to Florida: "They will have to kill me before those white shits in Florida take my house back. I would take a bullet for Fidel." Several informants made reference to the beating of Rodney King, insisting that such a thing would never happen in Cuba.

Cuba is clearly no racial paradise where prejudice, bigotry and the legacy of hundreds of years of slavery and racial inequality have been eliminated once and for all. However, communist Cuba has greatly reduced the importance of race as a social division. Much of the whitest or most European descended 10% of the population abandoned Cuba after the revolution; the rates of intermarriage between white and black greatly increased; and Fidel Castro officially declared that "we are an African-Latin nation." As an Afro-Cuban taxi driver told me, "in the past, when the whites had all the power, we worried ourselves about their attitudes and ideas. Now I don't care about racial attitudes. I have an equal right to housing, an equal right to a job, and an equal right to medical care. Yes, there are white Cubans who still say racist things, but those are just words and that is their problem, not mine." Virtually all Cubans agree that the Cuban revolution and the communist system has been very good for Afro-Cubans. The national claim, summed up nicely by an Afro-Cuban musician, that "Castro has done more for black people than any world leader in history," is one of the few things that most Cubans can agree on. This unprecedented levelling of political, economic, and social inequalities between black and white and the struggle to end racism in Cuba is so deeply tied in people's minds to Castro and communism that for many the coming collapse of communism in Cuba is seen as the automatic rebirth of racism, before it has even happened.

"The Special Period"

Cubans, who formerly enjoyed the highest standard of living in Latin America, based on heavily subsidized trade with the former communist countries, are currently facing a situation in which the basic necessities of life are no longer provided by the government. With the collapse of the Soviet Union and the end of the very favourable trade terms with the former countries of the Warsaw pact, Cuba has both been thrown abruptly into the world market and seen a massive effort on the part of the U.S. government to tighten the economic blockade. This has been accompanied by an increase in the extra-legal often violent activities of CIA connected anti-Castro Cubans against the island. All this has increasingly isolated the Cuban workers' state from any "international community" and produced a debilitating spiral downwards of virtually all Cuban economic indicators.

It is estimated that with the fall of the Soviet Union Cuba has lost one to two billion dollars per year in trade leading to a decline of roughly 50% in its gross social product since 1989. This massive and nearly overnight collapse in the Cuban standard of living has led to the grinding shortages and severe rationing that Fidel Castro has dubbed "the special period." Milk, meal, and fresh vegetables are unavailable through state stores for all but young children, diabetics, and others with special medical conditions. Consumer products like toothpaste, shampoo, and normal bar soap[3] have also disappeared from the state sector. Blackouts are frequent. The tap water is becoming less clean in certain areas and often does not run for several hours per day. Public transportation is greatly reduced and there are no longer luxuries from eastern Europe in the stores. The isolation from the rest of the world has led panicked Cuban professionals, like computer technicians, doctors, and engineers who are unable to read the latest journal articles, learn the new machines, or attend international conferences to fear that by the time the special period is over, they will have been left behind by their various professions. Life has simply become much more difficult and uncertain for most Cubans. The general fatigue, malaise, and crankiness pervading Cuban society led many Cubans to seek escape to the United States in the summer of 1994.

In response to this crisis, the government has opened the economy to tourism and joint economic ventures with foreign capitalists in hopes of replacing the lost international investment and spurring private production through market incentives. In 1993 the Cuban government legalized the holding of U.S. dollars for the first time since the 1960s. This effectively legalized the black market and threw many of the luxuries and basic commodities no longer on the shelves of state stores onto the open market in dollar stores and informal markets across Cuba. With little work available and a massive retreat of the state sector, "self-employment" has also been encouraged. At present 210,000 people are legally licensed by the national government to be "self-employed." But with dollars legal again it is certain that the numbers of people who work in

---

3   In special period Cuba the variety of soap that is generally provided by the government is very caustic and abrasive due to the shortage of enough oil to produce adequate soap.

various semi-legal informal sector enterprises is far larger and petty capitalism has grown throughout the island.

While the very barest necessities are still available to all the people through state stores, these bare necessities are hardly enough to survive on,[4] much less live a decent life. These privations are very difficult for Cubans who previously had the highest standard of living in Latin America. As one man put it "we Cubans don't have the normal Latin American expectations. We expect to live like people in the European countries." The problem is particularly difficult with regard to big-ticket consumer goods like kitchen appliances, air conditioners, televisions, and automobiles. No longer available through eastern European state sector industries at prices regulated by the government, these products arc now for sale to individual Cubans only through the dollar market. This is virtually impossible without access to foreign money, when the average monthly salary in the state sector is about $4 per month, regardless of profession. Virtually all Cubans now must find a way to obtain dollars. As they are discovering, to be a capitalist you need something to sell.

The elimination of prostitution was an early point of pride for the revolution. Now, back with a vengeance, it is one of the major tourist draws in Havana for the many European and South American men who come to Cuba for vacations. People rent out extra bedrooms to tourists, use their cars as both licensed and unlicensed taxis, and provide a wide variety of services to tourists and Cubans who have the dollars to pay for them. Except for the lucky few who either have jobs that force them into regular contact with tourists or who run some kind of business that captures a regular flow of dollars, for most Cubans, the dollar economy is extremely chaotic, unplanned, and random.

This policy of encouraging the growth of an internal capitalist economy has reintroduced into Cuban society many inequalities unseen since the early 1960s. Miramar, a neighbourhood of Havana where many of the more successful entrepreneurs are reputed to live, boasts nicely painted houses along well tended streets, with satellite dishes that sell U.S. cable television to residents of the community and dollar stores stocked with fax machines, Korean televisions, European washers and dryers, and a small supermarket with everything from European chocolate to powdered milk and German beer.

At the "Rapido," billed as genuine American-style fast food, red, white, and blue

---

4   An indicator of how low the Cuban rations actually are is that in 1993, the worst year of the special period, mass vitamin B deficiencies leading to temporary blindness were found in Cubans throughout the island. Unable to raise the rations of foods that provide vitamin B, the government instituted a program of regular distribution of B supplement tablets and injections throughout the inland.

mini-skirted waitresses on roller skates are paid in dollars to serve customers in their Polish, East German, and Soviet built cars, while women dressed in stylish imported clothing pose and local Havana businessmen strip off fifty dollar bills from wads of American money to pay for hot dogs and beer for whole tables filled with people. At night the nightclubs and restaurants fill up not just with Argentine, Spanish, and German men on sexual safari, but also with local Havana entrepreneurs who, in the absence of a genuine capitalist financial sector, have little to do with their money but spend it on wine, women, song, and that most desired of Cuban commodities, pow-dered milk. There is a wild west quality to the dollar economy that belies its small size.

While these little big men of the Cuban cash economy carry around large sums of money and act like "pre-revolution" mobsters, they currently represent an extremely fragile petty capitalist class. The relatively small sums that they are dealing in and the few opportunities for investment leave them with little power beyond having a somewhat more comfortable life and the ability to make their neighbours jealous. For many Cubans who do not have easy access to hot dogs or any form of meat and who work in the state sector at low wages that pay for the basics and "nada mas" these "dollar men" are the source of envy. However for many black Cubans they represent the possibility of their worst nightmare invading the island: American style racism.

Afro-Cubans and the Long Shadow of Rodney King

Black Cubans feel particularly vulnerable contemplating the change in the balance of forces away from the program of the Cuban revolution and toward attempts at integration with the capitalist world. Few Afro-Cubans have jobs in the tourist industry or relatives in the United States who send regular cash remittances, making it difficult to buy foreign-made products, act like big men at El Rapido, or go to clubs and tourist restaurants. Many Afro-Cubans talked of their fears of an "American solution." As an Afro-Cuban computer-technician told me, "If Cuba gets invaded by the Americans, we black Cubans will have no choice, we will have to fight to the death, every person. It is different for the others. They are faithful to their country and they know what a great leader Fidel is, but for us there is American racism. We know what happens to black people in the United States. We know what happened in Los Angeles with Rodney King and the police. We haven't had that here since before the revolution."

Cubans of every colour and background express their consciousness of the role of the United States in the global spread of racism. One often hears that "really it was the Americans we fought in Angola and not Africans." The neating of Rodney King, tho assassinations of Martin Luther King and Malcolm X, and the US. government support for pro-apartheid forces in Southern Africa stand as proof for many black Cubans that whatever privations Fidel and the communist system have in store for them are better than "what is out there."

While Cubans are highly sensitive to rare rotations outside Cuba, due in part to Cuban government propaganda and the evening news which is often filled with reports of police brutality and other forms of discrimination against blacks in the United States, they also recognize a rising consciousness of racial discrimination in Cuba. As one black Cuban, who was actually doing quite well as a bartender in a tourist hotel put it, "the S.A. after all these businesses (S.A.- Sociedad Anonimo is Spanish for anonymous partnership, a rough equivalent of the English 'Corp,'), it means *socios amigos* (friends for partners), you have to have those kind of *amigos*, like those whites in Miami." When I asked if there were better neighbourhoods in Havana where the buildings were not in a state of permanent disrepair, I was sent to Miramar, where "there are white people who watch American television and live well." Many black Cubans noting white people's differential access to international capital and networks believe that the white Cuban in Miami and U.S. businesses in general will reproduce the U.S. racial system in Cuba. An Afro-Cuban teenager nicely summed up this feeling of being "iced out" of the developing capitalist market: "Whites in the United States prefer to make business with whites here."

Several different people pointed out the differences in how black and white Cuban defectors were treated when they arrived in the United States. A black Cuban woman who works in the informal sector taking in sewing jobs whose ex-husband left Cuba during the Mariel[5] exodus said,

> when the white Cubans came to the United States, they were given welcome by the president and allowed to do whatever they wanted. When my husband went over there they were all locked up in prisons and camps and called criminals and lunatics – prejudice. That is why blacks in the United States like Fidel better than their own president."

In economically stressed "special period" Cuba, the poor welcome given to the

---

5   April of 1980 saw the first large-scale migration of black Cubans to the United States. Released during Jimmy Carter's pre-election war drum beating against Cuba, the U.S. government was caught by surprise at thousands of nonwhite refugees on their shores. Instead of standing by these people that they had encouraged to leave, they sought to blame Castro and portrayed the Marielitos as a group of mentally ill criminals, and other dregs of Cuban society that Castro had gotten rid of at U.S. expense. For many black Cubans this was an ugly slap in the face to the fathers, uncles, brothers and sons who had attempted to make the big journey that thad previously been made by white Cubans.

"*Marielitos*" has possibly permanent repercussions for the "on the ground" relationship between black Cubans and their non-black compatriots.

The simple fact that there were no sizable black Cuban immigrations to the United States until 1980 puts the entire Afro-Cuban community in the United States twenty years behind in the building of businesses, careers, and the accumulation of capital. This "late development" is further compounded by U.S. racism, the less affluent period in which they immigrated, the severe world economic downturn of 1982, and their stigmatization in U.S. public opinion. As a result, the *Marielitos* generally do not have enough money to send the kind of regular remittances back to the island that their white counterparts send. Furthermore, with each tightening of restrictions on the expatriating of U.S. money to Cuba, it becomes more difficult and expensive to help relatives on the island. This tends to reduce or even eliminate the remittances of the more recent and financially less secure *Marielitos*. Meanwhile, as white Cubans on the island circulate their remittances[6] and draw on foreign connections to obtain commodities for sale in the dollar economy, they show preferential hiring patterns in the rapidly growing dollar service economy.

A renewed racial differentiation threatens to consign black Cubans to the economic margins of the new Cuba. As only the most public face of this "new differentiation," an informal survey of the government-owned dollar stores in and around Western Havana showed that, with the exception of a parking lot attendant at El Rapido and a security guard at a dollar store, virtually none of the employees appeared to be Afro-Cuban. This confirmed what Afro-Cubans had told me about the heavily white character of the dollar economy. The legalization of dollars and the gradual liquidation of the state sector in favour of the private sector has therefore aided in the reproduction of U.S. racial inequalities in Cuba.

This Afro-Cuban identification of the external connection with increasing inequality and the feeling that there are only bad things waiting for them outside Cuba in the world of capitalism is the other side of the general belief among Cubans that the revolution benefitted Afro-Cubans the most of any group. It may partially explain why many black Cubans still put so much faith in Castro, in spite of the fact that it was he who introduced the market reforms. As almost everyone in Cuba says, "with the fall of the socialist camp Fidel has no choice."

---

6   It is currently estimated that roughly 40% of the foreign money coming to Cuba is in the form of remittances. Some estimates put it at nearly one half billion dollars per year. With the collapse of the state sector after the fall of the Soviet Union these remittances and the people who receive them become more and more important in Cuban society.

Afro-Cuban Youth: Between Communism and Capitalism

The U.S. press has recently featured reports of a generation gap in Cuba. It is commonly said that young people with no memory of the revolution and the way things were before the revolution are completely uninterested in communism and only want more consumer goods and to be plugged into international youth culture. This MTV-as-apple-of-knowledge argument seems very compelling on the surface. In fact, many young Cubans have little interest in communism, little patience with Castro and his "tasks of the revolution," and a tremendous desire to be connected to "what's happening out there" instead of being trapped on this slowly starving island with its rapidly unraveling political culture.

However, this lack of commitment to communism that many U.S. commentators have noticed among Cuban youth appears to be due more to their ignorance of the possibilities that their parents had in the 1960s, 1970s, and 1980s than their not knowing how bad it was before communism. Young people who are just beginning their adulthood have little ability to imagine themselves fitting into a system that offers nothing but the promise of extended crisis and waste of their youthful energy.

While there are certainly many young people of all backgrounds who have recently finished school and are beginning their work life in the state sector with much enthusiasm and a strong loyalty to the still two million person communist party, for many youth there are few appealing possibilities for employment at wages that only purchase the meager state supplies in the rapidly shrinking economy. The lack of opportunities in the special period to travel to Eastern Europe, Africa, or other Latin American countries to be educated or participate in professional, military, or humanitarian activities is yet another loss of incentive to work within the system. There was a time in the not-so-distant past when good grades in school might get a student sent to a university in East Germany, a humanitarian project in Latin America, or a conference on the beach in Bulgaria. It is not so much the restrictions of the system that seem to make young people impatient with communism and yearn for the glitter of U.S. capitalism, but its loss of ability to provide economic incentive, rewards for achievement, or project the romantic image of a viable national project as it did in the past.

Despite their political education and apparent consciousness of U.S. racism, black Cuban youth are no exception to this "new alienation." They know about prejudice against blacks in the United States but they see people with relatives in Miami and New Jersey getting satellite antennas, washing machines, and other luxuries that are no longer provided by the state. They see the government laying off thousands of people[7] and paying those who are employed starvation wages. Many of them would rather take their chances in a society that has the potential to reward their energies and efforts than in a society where misery, idleness, starvation, and increasing inequality await them. As one Afro-Cuban man of 18 years old told me, "I do not believe in God or the Devil or any of those religious things. This is the only life I have and I am dying here on this prison island. I would do anything to get to the United States." Another young black Cuban who had displayed a strong knowledge of the history of blacks in the United States and the U.S. repression of the Black Panther Party told me that his dream was to go to the United States and start a business, "because there is nothing to do here, but wait." He felt that in spite of the racism in the United States he would have more opportunity to succeed "where there are many opportunities for many people, than here where there are few opportunities and the government is thoroughly corrupt."

Many young Afro-Cuban women who have turned to prostitution feel that the government and the system has a lot less to offer them than the foreign tourists with their shiny cameras and easy ability to buy a chicken dinner or drink *mojitos* (the Cuban national mixed drink) in a $100 per night hotel. They see that black Cubans are not the ones who are managing the dollar enterprises and they would rather cast their lot with foreigners than wait for segregation and colour stratification to slowly return to the island and strangle them. As a young professional woman who made extra money in the evenings "getting to know foreign men" told me, "I am mixed and my friend is a black and many foreigners think we are unusual and will give us more."

For many young people in Cuba between 15 and 25 who see no viable future, have increasingly distant memories of life before the special period, and know little else but privations and defeats, the stories of money, success, glamour and glitter in the land of capitalism beyond their shores fires their imaginations.

Afro-Cubans Between the Sword and the Wall

Afro-Cubans look at the disintegration of the Cuban revolution and feel themselves to be "between the sword and the wall." In this case the sword is the sword of

---

7   In 1995 the Cuban government announced the end of full employment and the right to a job. While this legal change does not represent a major change in the current lives of Cubans who are still provided with food, housing, education, and health care by the government, it has some major repercussions for the future. It could be seen as a major step in laying the basis for a full-blown capitalist economy, with a competitive labour market and a reserve army of labour. When one looks at the proportion of African descended peoples in the Americas who are consigned to this fate by capitalist economies it is not unreasonable to imagine this same fate for Black Cubans in a capitalist Cuban society. One of the fundamental tenets of Marxism-Leninism as it is both theorized and has been practiced is the notion that everyone, regardless of abilities, has both the right to work and the obligation to work. In this quiet way Cuba has retreated from one of the most basic aspects of its system.

U.S. racism and the system of racial inequality that they had hoped they had left behind in 1959. The wall is the weakness of the isolated Cuban economy and the fragmentation of the collective state system into which they have invested massive amounts of labour and political support. While a few Afro-Cubans articulated a kind of pan-African nationalism, most of my informants were much more worried about day-to-day problems such as getting powdered milk or new clothing that is not provided by the state stores and finding a way to pay for it. They saw that while there is still a rough equality for the majority of people in the state sector, in the increasingly important private sector inequality rapidly grows. They attribute this to "corruption" rampant within the government and the power white Cubans have to mobilize "pre-revolutionary" resources and networks. In the words of a black Cuban woman who teaches judo in the state sector,

> the best businessmen here are whites. The whites have the rich families in Miami, the whites have the business knowledge, the whites have the connections in the United States that this corrupt government wants. Of course the whites run all the businesses here, they do it because they can do it and the government needs them to do it.

Thus old divisions are causing new inequalities.

While the policies of Fidel Castro are directly leading to this "new inequality" in which not everybody starts with an equal opportunity to become a capitalist, it seems likely that Castro can still count on black Cubans to provide a central pillar of support for his policies, his government, and his bloated military apparatus. These changes have the contradictory effect of both alienating many black Cubans, as citizens with less recourse to the private economy, from some of the most important trends in contemporary Cuban society and yet driving them deeper into defending the government that is promoting these changes that do not seem to be in their interests. This contradictory position seems to be pretty well understood as a "tactical retreat" by those black Cubans who do remember pre-revolutionary racism or grew up after the revolution. As one black Cuban woman of about thirty, who was working part-time as a prostitute for the tourists told me, "my grandparents didn't even know how to read or write and look at me, I am a chemist and I know Russian. These are things the revolution has given us that cannot be put into numbers or statistics. If Fidel has to follow the rules of the market for a time, ok, he has no choice."

However, most young black Cubans, like virtually all Cuban youth, have little patience with the whole business of adjustments, tactics, and the protection of a revolution that has given them little and pours their youth down a hopeless geo-political sinkhole. They have heard stories of incredible riches and high wages. They have heard the music, seen the movies, and watched the television shows of the millionaires of the US. African diaspora. Many Cuban teenagers follow U.S. professional sports and have seen the glamour, wealth and opportunities that are enjoyed by U.S. black athletes whose only athletic competition in this hemisphere are Cubans. For many Cubans it is a point of pride that "U.S, heavy weight boxers made millions of dollars throughout the 1970s and 1980s and none of them could beat Teofilo Stevenson," the great Cuban Olympic boxer, who was reputed to be the best fighter in the world throughout much of the 70s and 80s. Cubans watch U.S. baseball on TV, listen to sports on U.S. radio, and become very excited about the Pan-American games, in which all Latin American countries participate, but where every event amounts to a competition between Cuba and the U.S. for the gold and silver medals.

During the 1995 Pan-American games Cubans were quick to point out that "their boys and girls" were beating future millionaires. Although Cuba won more total medals than nearly all of the other Latin American countries put together, they were sorely disappointed that the United States had taken more medals in contrast to the previous Pan-American games in which Cuba had beaten the U.S. Between the identification of U.S. sports being dominated by African Americans and the popularity of African Americam music, many Afro-Cuban youth, regardless of their ideological leanings view U.S. African Americans as dynamic producers of culture and excellence in sports. They see them as a group that in spite of racial prejudice has accumulated more wealth and has a higher standard of living than any other African peoples in the Americas. For a young person who sees no future in Cuba and has been lied to over and over again by a corrupt government and a megalomaniacal leader, the "American dream" is something to live for and a way to "get on with your life." They want to go to the United States and get a jump on the world of capitalism, which everybody including Fidel seems to suggest in one way or another will come to Cuba anyhow.

Conclusion: Racism as a Transnational Process

The function of racism, to divide black and white workers, both to reduce their bargaining power over wages and as a means of political control is still very much the foundation on which local systems of racism are based. However, the contemporary capitalist world system is based on an unequal distribution of wealth and resources and an international division of labour in which "blackness" or "non-whiteness" is a transnational category that divides society on more than a local basis. The diffusion of these transnational divisions brutally reproduces inequalities and the justifications for them around the globe. These inequalities have many different sources: the reinforcement of ancient prejudices; the political, economic, and cultural links between Third-World ruling classes and North Atlantic economies and societies; the still very non-black character of U.S. business; the world predominance of U.S. media; preferential access to doing business with a U.S. military base or firm; and the historic legacy of inequalities produced by the African slave system of the Americas.

However, the U.S. "black question" is becoming both the metaphor for articulating difference and the organizational principle for implementing that difference as it is diffused throughout the world. This dominant political, economic, and cultural role has increased with the spread of satellite technologies and the collapse of the Soviet counterweight to U.S. domination, homogenizing culture and ideology. This "new world order" in which "blackness" represents an international division in the world working class that is becoming more transnational has the potential to become increasingly universal as more isolated and peripheral or previously closed sections of the world are integrated into "the new world order."

Regardless of how much inequality has developed in contemporary Cuba, Afro-Cubans articulate a very clear message. They are apprehensive about the coming changes and fear racial injustice tied to the notion of an international category of race or "blackness." Just as the anti-Latino law in California entitled "Proposition 187" has become a famous symbol of U.S. prejudice and bigotry throughout *mestizo* Latin America, there are whole countries and regions of the world particularly here in the Americas over which hang the long shadow of Rodney King blocking the sun.

References

The Black Scholar
   1985   Roundtable on the History of Racial Prejudice in Cuba. January: 36.
Bourgois, Philippe
   1989   Ethnicity at Work: Divided Labor on a Central American Banana Plantation. Baltimore: Johns Hopkins University Press.
Brenner, Philip, ed.
   1989   The Cuba Reader: The Making of a Revolutionary Society. NY: Grove Press.
Carneado, Jose Felipe
   1962   *La discriminación racial en Cuba no volverá jamas*. Cuba Socialista. La Habana: Minrex.
Casal, Lourdes
   1979   Race Relations in Contemporary Cuba. *In* Anani Dzidzienyo and Lourdes Casal. The Position of Blacks in Brazil and Cuban Society. London: Minority Rights Group.
Fagen, Richard
   1969   The Transformation of Political Culture in Cuba. Stanford, Ca.: Stanford University Press.
Fernandez, Nadine T.
   1996   The Color of Love: Young Interracial Couples in Cuba. Latin American Perspectives 23 (Winter).
Fuente, Alejandro de la
   1995   Race and Inequality in Cuba 1899-1981. Journal of Contemporary History 30.
Glazer, Jon
   1992   Working for the Tourist Dollar. The Nation 254 (June 15): 820.
Habel, Janette
   1991   Cuba the Revolution in Peril. London: Verso.
Mintz, Sidney W.
   1992   The Birth of African-American Culture: An Anthropological Perspective. Boston: Beacon Press.
Moore, Carlos
   1988   Castro, the Blacks and Africa. Los Angeles: Center for Afro-American Studies, University of California.

Serviat, Pedro

    1986   *El problema negro en Cuba y su solucion definitiva.* La Habana: Editora Politica.

Taber, Michael, ed.

    1983   Fidel Castro Speeches: Our Power Is That of the Working People. New York: Pathfinder Press.

Zeitlin, Maurice

    1967   Revolutionary Politics and the Cuban Working Class. Princeton: Princeton University Press.

Part Two

Identity, Belief, and Inequality

INDIAN OR WHITE?
Racial Identities in the
British Columbian Fishing Industry[1]

Charles R. Menzies

Introduction

It's late in the evening and the five-man fishing crew has just crowded into the boat's small galley. Everyone is tired but jubilant. The boat is nearly full of salmon and by early tomorrow morning should be headed to town fully loaded. It has been the kind of a day fishermen dream of.

After a hurried meal the men begin to relax. A bottle of liquor is brought to the table. Each man pours himself a drink. Talk of the day's fishing turns to remembrances of the: past. I sip my drink and listen as the skipper begins to tell a story.

"It was the end of August, 1953," says Robert Bruce. "I was up at John McNab's place. Evert Jones from Canadian Fish – he was the fleet manager – asked McNab if he wanted a job running a company seine boat. We were between things right then. What with the fishing shut down up north we had nothing to do. 'If yah got a place for Bob here,' McNab said, I'll do it.'"

The three men passed a half empty rum bottle around and the deal was done: "All you gotta do," Jones told the two men "is go out to Port Edward [a small town a

1   My thanks to Anthony Marcus – friend, colleague, and comrade in arms – for his ongoing commentary on my work and for the hours of discussions we have engaged in. Thanks is also due to Dr. Gerald M. Sider for his continued support and advice. A special thanks to "Robert Bruce" and "Scott Mills" for being patient storytellers and considerate sources throughout my ongoing work on the pressing problems of the First Nations people.

few miles from Prince Rupert] and pick up a seiner. Get it all rigged, pick up a crew, and I want you boys to go down to the Straits for the fall dogs."[2]

At the boat Bruce and McNab found a family from a nearby Indian village living on the boat. The man and his family had fished the boat for close to ten years. They didn't own the boat but when the company had first hired him it had been accepted practice to allow a skipper and his family to live on the boat in the off season. But now, because of a decision made over a bottle of rum, Bruce was carrying the man and his family's belongings off the boat.

"That Indian guy just stood watching, crying. He tried to get us to leave everything on the boat, to go away. He told us that he needed a place to live. McNab told him 'It's just a job.'"

As the skipper talked he refilled our glasses. He paused, took a sip and continued his story:

"It was a hard thing to do. The old man could have been my grandfather, an uncle. Times change. Fishing changes and the company didn't want the boat tied up to the dock rotting away. They wanted the boat out fishing. That Indian guy didn't want to leave the north. But he didn't own the boat. It wasn't his decision to make and once he refused to take the boat south the company gave McNab a chance to run it. That's it. You either work or you lose out. I wanted to work."[3]

Robert Bruce's grandfather, Jonah Mills, a named hereditary chief from a north coast Tsimshian village, was in fact related to the family thrown off the fishing boat that night. In the space created by the passage of time Robert Bruce remembers the event with sadness. I have heard this story told many times and in several variations. Yet the fundamental moral remains: the "Indian" fisher was unwilling to adapt, he was an anachronism in a modern world. Robert Bruce desperately wanted to move into that modern world and in so doing became "white."

Since its inception in the late 1880s, the commercial fishery in British Columbia has been characterized by myriad ethnic, racial, and regional divisions and alliances. Out of this cauldron of ethnic diversity the racial identities "white" and "Indian"

---

2   The Straits is a reference to the long channel between Vancouver Island and the mainland called Johnstone Strait that runs from Campbell River on the south to Alert Bay on the north. Fall dogs refers to chum salmon caught in the months from September to November.

3   The man evicted by McNab and Bruce was caught by the changes then occurring in the industry. Up until then most of the fishing was regionally based. The companies owned boats which fished in set areas and when the local salmon runs were over the boats were tied to the dock until the next fishing season. In many cases, as in this example, the skipper and his family would be allowed a limited use of the vessel in the off season. However, as corporate control became more and more centralized redundant vessels were scrapped and the existing fleet was deployed to take advantage of as much fishing time as possible. Skippers who didn't want to change their fishing styles were unceremoniously dumped.

emerged. Being "Indian," "white," "Asian," man or women continues to play a determining role in individual experiences and life opportunities; rules are not as firmly fixed as one might assume. The following illustration is as much a history of how a family has been cut apart by capital as it is a story about the creation and reproduction of race. This story focuses on two cousins: one, Robert Bruce, white; the other, Scott Mills, Indian. The life histories of these two men were collected in the course of fieldwork on the interaction between First Nation and Euro-Canadian fishers within the highly charged context of First Nations land claims (Menzies 1994). Their history simultaneously unites them as kin while segregating them by race. My aim in recounting their story is to highlight the historical processes that create such racial-ethnic identities.[4]

The Development of the Resource Extraction Industries

Underlying many analyses of ethnicity or race is an essentialist assumption: ethnic groups are static and unchanging. Once created, they are always there until the homogenizing force of state power erases their uniqueness. In practice the expansion and consolidation of state power both destroys and creates ethnic variation (Sider 1993).[5] The origins of ethnic groups are often found in brief moments of demographic dislocation or conquest. Their historical trajectory is not determined at the moment of their creation. Rather, it is shaped by the enduring day-today struggle over the changing ways in which ethnic identity is used to structure, limit or privilege access to resources at the local level.

On the northwest coast of British Columbia, Canada, people of European and First Nations descent have come together and separated over the years as the result of the historical movement of capital. Initial contact revolved around the "cash nexus," the exchange of commodities such as fur, iron, beads, or other trade goods. As European settlement extended into First Nations territories, marriages between Euro-Canadian businessmen and First Nations women became increasingly common. According to several commentators, these early marriages followed customary First Nations practices and were ostensibly designed to facilitate trade and cooperation between groups (Fisher 1977).

---

4   In this analysis I focus on a decidedly male point of view. Historically, anthropologists did not consider the implications of the gender of their respondents when writing about the fieldwork experience. For the most part, both anthropologist and respondent were male. Today it is widely acknowledged that gender plays an important role in shaping our lives and structuring our experiences (see, for example, Moore 1988).

5   The creation of the Métis on the Canadian prairies is a case in point. The Métis emerged as a people at the point of contact between the indigenous peoples and the incoming Europeans during the early fur trading period (see Wolf 1982).

The extension of industrial capitalism into this region fundamentally altered the basis of alliance. No longer valued as trading partners, First Nations were slotted into the developing resource economy as a subordinate part of the growing industrial labour force in which workers were segregated by race and gender. Union organizers and social activists have attempted with little success to overcome these structural divisions.

In British Columbia, a maritime-based fur trade structured the early contacts between Europeans and First Nations (1774-1858). In this period a European-based mercantile capitalism articulated with an indigenous kin-ordered mode of production,[6] in which the control of labour power and the production of trade goods remained under the control of the native American traders who were for the most part "chiefs." They "mobilized their followers and personal contacts to deliver ... otter skins, and [their] power grew concomitantly with the development of the trade" (Wolf 1982:185). The merging of these two modes of production – one based on the family and one based on European capitalism – produced new wealth and intense inflation for both First Nations and Europeans (Fisher 1977:18-20; Codere 1961:443-467; Wolf 1982:186-192). However, as Europeans prospered from this fur trade and developed modern industry, First Nations people lost control over trade and were displaced by a settler-based industrial capitalism.

Vancouver Island and British Columbia began the change from colonies in which Europeans exploited indigenous manpower to colonies of settlement in the 1850s following the discovery of gold in the interior of the province. With the exception of the fishing industry, First Nations labour power "was only of marginal significance in the economic concerns of the Europeans" (Fisher 1977:96, 109). Mining, forestry, and fishing supplanted the fur trade and became the backbone of British Columbia's economy. By the mid-1880s indigenous control of land and resources was almost completely destroyed. At the same time First Nations people became integrated "into virtually every major resource industry in [British Columbia] as workers and owner-operators" (Knight 1978: 10). Throughout the period of industrialization and until the early 1970s they were workers on fishing boats, and in fishplants, mills, and logging camps, Consequently, First Nations and non-aboriginal people were allies throughout most of the early twentieth century in class politics such as trade unionism that de-emphasized tribal allegiances.

Alliances between First Nations and non-aboriginal fishers have played a major role in shaping British Columbia's union movement in the fishing industry (Knight

---

6   The kin-ordered mode of production is one in which access to and control of labour power is mediated by relations of kinship. For an elaboration of this concept see Wolf (1982:88-96).

1978:78). On the north coast First Nations fishers and cannery workers supplied the bulk of the early labour force. In 1896, 1897, and again in 1899, they played a prominent role in central and north coast fish strikes (Knight 1978:96-97). First Nations people were also decisive in turning the tide in favour of the Fishermen's Union in a critical strike on the Fraser River in 1900.

That Fraser River strike was important for two major reasons: it demonstrated that a multi-racial (ethnic) labour force could work together toward a common goal, and "for the first time, the canners had been forced to concede a share of their economic wealth to their employees" (Meggs 1991:66). After nearly thirty years of expansion, the industrial canning industry was an almost invincible force. Until the 1900 strike the large processing firms had dictated nearly all terms of employment, prices of fish, and conditions of work. Following the strike, however, the canning industry was confronted by a union movement that had transcended racial, gender, and regional bounds to act collectively in their own interests as workers.

This early example of multi-racial union building was part of an overall mobilization sweeping across the Pacific northwest. Swirling within this new unionism were tendencies as diverse as the syndicalism of the "Wobblies," the social fabianism of the traditional labour movement, and the more radical revolutionary socialism of the Second International Socialist Parties of Canada, British Columbia, and the United States. As opposed to the earlier craft unionism in which workers would join unions or guilds that only represented one particular craft (such as teamsters, carpenters, or masons), these new unions aimed to organize the entire working class under the umbrella of "One Big Union" whose ultimate goal was to overthrow their capitalist bosses and introduce workers' control. From our vantage point today such a goal may appear utopian. In the early decades of the twentieth century, however, the possibility of working-class revolution was not an idle dream. In the general strikes in Seattle, Winnipeg, and Toronto, the workers uprisings in Germany, Hungary, and Italy, and the revolution in Russia, open class warfare was the order of the day.

Union building in the fishing industry was most intense in the 1890s-1910s (led by the Second International Socialist Party of Canada) and in 1925-45 (led by the Communist Party of Canada). Organizers worked hard at building labour unions that included both First Nations and non-aboriginal. Although they were accepting of First Nations self-organization, most union organizers believed that First Nations people's interests were with the working class in general. In fact, from the 1890s until the depression of the 1930s First Nations fishers opted to join the unions rather than organizing separately (Knight 1978:96-97; Meggs 1991:41-42, 62-70;

Pinkerton 1992262; Clement 1986:38) They did not begin to organize separately until the mid-1930s. An important "turning point was the 1936 Rivers Inlet strike, viewed by white union fishermen as a major advance but recalled to this day in native communities as a serious betrayal" (Meggs 1991:155; see also Clement 1986:38, and Gladstone 1953:32).

The conflict between Euro-Canadian and First Nations union members was in part a product of the respective fishers' home ports and the differing extent to which their entire families were involved in the fishery. A great many of the Euro-Canadians fishers lived in Vancouver. Each season they would ready their boats, leave their families behind and set sail for fishing grounds spread along the coast. First Nations fishers, on the other hand, mostly fished in or close to their historic territories. More often than not their entire family laboured in the fishery either as fishers or shoreworkers. In the Rivers Inlet strike, First Nations fishers were concerned about the well-being of their families locked away behind picket lines: "We weren't allowed to go up to Knight Inlet to see our wives and children and we wanted to know how they were getting along. They finally settled it but we didn't make hardly anything at all because we had been tied up nearly all season" (James Sewid, quoted in: Meggs 1991:155). Following this incident the Pacific Coast Native Fishermen's Association was formed at Alert Bay on the south coast which later amalgamated with the north coast Native Brotherhood of British Columbia to form one unified coast-wide organization (Clement 1986:95; Meggs 1991:154-5).

The social impetus that gave rise to the Native Brotherhood emerged out of the trade union movement's inability to deal effectively with the problem of racism. Though union organizers attempted to include them in pan-racial organizations, First Nations fishers ultimately found themselves in conflict with many of their Euro-Canadian coworkers. The major point of contention between non-aboriginal and First Nations fishers was the issue of land claims. Despite their common confrontation with capital as workers, they never developed a united policy on redressing the theft of First Nations territories and Euro-centric attacks against First Nations social institutions. While unions addressed some aspects of First Nations experiences as workers, they seemed incapable of confronting the racism and segregation of the new industrial society that was emerging in British Columbia.

(Re)Producing Race in the Colonial Encounter

The struggle of First Nations people to regain control of their traditional land and resources brings them into conflict with non-aboriginals employed in resource extraction industries such as fishing. Non-aboriginals anticipate the loss of their jobs and the end of their way of life. First Nations people look forward to a better tomorrow in which they again control their traditional territories. Although media and political attention given to First Nations land claims issues have increased, "public understanding of these developments has lagged far behind the amount of information bring disseminated" (Dyck 1986:32). These different expectations and understandings of the issues and the potential futures arise out of a particular socio-economic history in which "whites" and "Indians" have been functionally segregated according to the needs of capital.

Initially canneries relied upon an indigenous labour force, especially in the north of the province. Cannery managers would contract with local village or house leaders to hire entire families much in the same way as trading alliances had been organized during the fur trade period. This system quickly broke down in the south of the province under the onslaught of Euro-Canadian-American settlement. It remained the dominant mode of labour recruitment in the north and central coast, however, until the 1950s when "changes in labour supply, in markets for fish, in technology, and in government regulation rendered Indians less central to fishing and eventually to fish processing" (Newell 1993:206).

In their role as labour brokers for the canneries some First Nations leaders became part of a system of social differentiation in which they were able to accumulate wealth and assume names of higher rank. On the north coast, for example, motorized boats were not allowed in the gillnet fishery until 1923: "With the restrictions removed, the leading Indians purchased their own boats, often using their control of the labour supply in the competitive market to extract loans for the purpose from the cannery owners" (Tennant 1990:73).

Though some aboriginal "chiefs" thereby raised sufficient capital to purchase their own boats and then break free from the companies, most First Nations fishers could not. The reasons for this reflect the colonial relationship between the Canadian state and First Nations. Legal restrictions prevented First Nations fishers from borrowing money from banks, keeping them tied to the processing companies through debt. Changing fisheries management regulations and technological innovation combined, moreover, to push up the cost of operation, driving First Nations fishers out of the fishery (see, for example, McDonald 1994).

Fishers of European descent faced an entirely different set of conditions. While there were no legal barriers designed to prevent them from securing a loan to buy a fishing boat, the fish companies were able to maintain effective control over the

Euro-Canadian fishers through a monopoly-like control of fish prices. As opposed to their First Nations brethren, Euro-Canadian fishers could not fall back upon subsistence base or home village in times of need. Most resource workers of European descent circulated between jobs in forestry, fishing, construction, or other semi-skilled industrial jobs. Their only effective resistance against exploitation within the market economy was collective organization, as in trade unions, co-operatives, or credit unions. A vital co-operative and credit union movement in the Euro-Canadian communities following the Second World War created an avenue of escape for white fishers. Once out from under the economic control of the companies, an independent boat-owning class of predominately Euro-Canadian fishers developed. The longest lasting of these was the Prince Rupert Fishermen's Co-operative Association which in its heyday had a membership of more than 2,000 fishers and employed 500 workers in its Prince Rupert processing plant.

The fish canning industry in British Columbia has always relied upon a racially segregated workforce. While this produced immediate and pronounced benefits for the companies and their distant shareholders, it has not been in the best interests of either the First Nations or Euro-Canadian communities. The different historical links of Euro-Canadian and First Nations to the fishing industry has led to the current segregation of the fleet. First Nations fishers are more highly concentrated in the north and among the gillnet fleet. White fishers, though by no means absent in the gillnet fleet, predominate in the more capital intensive seine and offshore troll fleets. It is against this backdrop that the family history of Robert Bruce and Scott Mills must be read.

The Family Connection

The two main characters in this illustration are related as family through one man: Jonah Mills, a named hereditary Tsimshian chief.[7] Jonah Mills' own life reflects many of the changes occurring in the aboriginal world in his time. Born in the early 1860s, he was orphaned at an early age during one of the last battles within First Nations. In his early adolescence he went to live with a kinswoman and her Irish common-law husband in an Euro-Canadian settlement on the Skeena River. For most of his working life (approximately 1880 to 1920), Jonah Mills worked as a

---

7   Among the Coast Tsimshian people traditional property ownership is vested in "names" which are theoretically passed down matrilineally. Actual practice can be very different. Especially during the early part of this century the succession of names did not necessarily follow previous practice (see, for example: Garfield 1939 where she talks about the conflicts between Euro-Canadian inheritance laws and local laws and the problems of finding heirs). The importance of names reside in the fact that they actually embody a form of legal entitlement to real resources and their utilization.

wage labourer in the northern sawmill industry. During this period he accumulated sufficient capital to purchase a gas-powered boat which he used to transport trading goods and supplies between north coast First Nations villages.

Robert Bruce, born in 1929, is Jonah Mills' grandson. Bruce's mother was one of four daughters from Mills' first marriage in 1894 to a Tsimshian woman called Sarah. All four daughters married Euro-Canadian men and subsequently were "de-registered" and lost their status as "Indians" as defined by the then existing Indian Act of the federal government. Scott Mills, born in 1923, is Jonah Mills' son from his second marriage to a Tlingit woman in the 1920s.

By aboriginal custom of the time, all of Mills' children and grandchildren from both marriages would have had rights to membership in a specific house and clan (Garfield 1939) and potentially rights to a named position. Under Canadian law, however, only the children of the second marriage were granted Indian status. As a result the grandchildren from Mills' first family were legally non-Indian though their cultural identity was somewhat more ambiguous.

Though Robert Bruce and Scott Mills are closely related, they are essentially members of two separate communities segregated by racial identity. Robert Bruce is tied to the circuits of exchange and social networks that socially and economically define him as "white." He owns a modern seiner/longliner; for the most part he employs white crewmen; and he fishes for an organization opposed to First Nations land claims and a separate aboriginal fishery. Scott Mills is firmly entrenched in the "Indian" sector of the fishery. He mobilizes support and labour from within the First Nations community for his projects but lacks the individual capital required to gain access to the "white" business world.

This is not to say that the two men do not interact, share friends, or have business associates in common; they do. But, irrespective of their ancestry, one is part of the "Indian" world and the other the "white" world. Bruce's and Mills' cultural identities imply more than simply degrees of membership in "racially" defined communities. They reflect and have implications for the ways in which "Indian" and "white" families have become involved in the fishing industry.

While a few First Nations people are involved as owner-operators of the larger fishing vessels (see, for example, Knight 1978, Spradly/Sewid 1969, and Inglis/Assu 1969), in identity and how it is played out in the shape and reproduction of the fishery, "white" fishers behave in certain ways and "Indian" fishers in different ways. This division is reinforced (if not created) by federal government licensing policies that once excluded First Nations fishers by creating the food fish category in the late

1800s and then in recent years by creating special native licenses (see, for example, Newell 1993). There are broad class differences as well.

Robert Bruce

Robert Bruce was surprised by the number of First Nations people at his mother's funeral in 1942. He knew his grandfather Jonah was "Indian" but had a poor understanding of his First Nations heritage. As an adult looking back on his mother's funeral he speaks in wonderment: "They came from all over to pay their respects to her and my grandfather. At the time all I could think was all these Indians. They all came up to me at the end of the funeral and shook my hand. My grandfather had wanted an Indian funeral. He wanted to take her and bury her in his village. My father said 'no, no way.' He didn't want none of that. 'She didn't marry an Indian,' my father told Jonah Mills, 'she married me.'"

A few days after the funeral Jonah Mills approached his white son-in-law and asked for permission to take Robert Bruce to live with him in the village, so that he could be groomed as Mills' heir; but his white son-in-law refused.

Robert Bruce had one other opportunity to live with his grandfather. A few years after the funeral Robert Bruce left school to work in a northern fishplant. At that time Jonah Mills invited Bruce to come live with him and work on the family beach seine, located about seventy miles out of Prince Rupert in Jonah Mills' hereditary territory. In an interview Bruce said: "I wish I'd have gone. It'd have been good experience but I had a job that paid good money and I didn't want to lose it."

Robert Bruce's life in the 1950s and 1960s was like many other Euro- Canadian men in the resource industries: he moved from job to job as the need arose. He skippered a seine boat in 1955, and in 1957 he was hired to run a halibut schooner owned by his father's boss, a local ship-chandler and fish broker. In a fashion typical to many of his colleagues he settled down after his marriage to a Euro-Canadian woman in the early 1960s and took a deck-job on a high earning combination halibut-herring fishboat.

He bought his first boat, a fifty-five foot combination halibut longliner-salmon seiner, in 1967 with a loan from the local credit union. For the most part he has only hired crewmen of European origins. The few First Nations fishers who have worked for him were relatives. As a boat owner he became involved in a local fishermen's organization best know for its hardline stance against land claims and for its refusal to recognize union-called fish strikes.

Though he has lived for most of his life in the Prince Rupert region, he sees little of his "cousin" Scott Mills. The two men will on occasion meet each other on the street or in a cafe but for the most part they live in social worlds that do not overlap in any meaningful way.

Scott Mills

Scott Mills' life, though parallel to his cousin's, reflects the differences of his "Indian" identity. Scott's childhood and early adulthood was structured by life in his father's village, by customs that limited his choice of wife, and by the legal restrictions that inhibited his ability to own real estate, raise a loan from a chartered bank, or vote. However, as Jonah Mills' heir he had a name of power in his community.

Scott Mills operated his family's beach seine until the federal Department of Fisheries and Oceans to closed down in the 1960s. He then ran a company-owned gillnetter on the Skeena River during the summer sockeye season. When the company sold its gillnet fleet in the early 1980s he purchased the boat he was then running.

His marriage to a Tsimshian woman from a nearby village followed the protocols of an historic treaty between their respective "houses."[8] When Scott Mills took on his hereditary name he assumed the paramount position both in his house and in his village. As a hereditary chief he rose to prominence in the local Native Brotherhood and worked toward establishing a council of hereditary chiefs.

Circuits of Capital and Racial Identity

Over the course of the last century and a half industrial capitalism has become the defining system of global production. In its wake local cultures have been destroyed and re-created. In the Americas racial and ethnic identities (such as "Indian," "White," "Black," and "Chicano") have emerged out of a colonial encounter that threw together Africans, Europeans, and First Nations. On a macro-scale the form of political organization and the creation and reproduction of racial identities have been shaped by the colonial process and the development of capitalism. We may speak with ease and familiarity of the colonial process and the manner by which Spanish, British, French, American, Canadian, and other Euro-centric regimes

---

8   The house is the basic unit of kinship and political and economic activity amongst the Tsimshian. In terms of kinship a house is a matrilineage of people so closely related that the members know how they are related. It it the house that owns property and access to this property is determined through a ranked system of hereditary names distributed through the feast or potlatch system.

wrongfully expropriated First Nations land. However, the brute economic reality of this picture leaves aside the trickier and touchier questions of how cultural identities were reshaped, transformed, and re-created in the colonial process.

Along the borderlands of the North American settler society capitalism has been engaged in a spatial and cultural restructuring of racial, ethnic, and local identities. In this processes identities have not simply been imposed, they arise in a context of resistance and accommodation.

European merchants in the fur trade grafted their own capitalist economic system onto the indigenous kinship based system of labour control and surplus extraction. In the transition to industrial capitalism these prior relations allowed for the creation of a divided industrial workforce, with important consequences for both "white" and "Indian" kin-networks.

Robert Bruce and Scott Mills' family histories outline how two men of essentially similar origins have been socially assigned different racial identities. These identities were not set at birth. Many factors intervened to shape and structure who became "white" and who became "Indian." Both men made choices within the social bounds established by a system of production that relies to this day upon a racially segregated workforce. Their choices are limited and the penalties for transgression are severe. For Bruce the assimilationist policies of the Canadian state denied him the legal status of "Indian" while simultaneously denying Scott Mills the right to vote or borrow money from a bank.

In his act of throwing his "Indian" kin off the seine boat, Bruce participates in a system that relies upon racial segregation to function and in so doing becomes irrevocably "white." At one point in his life he had an opportunity to chose a different path, to join his grandfather and live with him. Bruce chooses to be "white," to be modern and take a job in the cash economy. To do otherwise would be to turn his back on what he saw as "the modem world." The dehumanizing logic of capital forced and manipulated Bruce into a position in which he threw his kinfolk off a boat and out of work. In 'becoming white" he became part of the shock troops of capital and implicated himself in the European appropriation of this land.

Scott Mills also made choices within the social limits of his life. He accepted the customs of his house and honoured their past treaties through his marriage. He would not have been alone if he had refused to follow custom. Many First Nations people have selected spouses who would have traditionally been considered either a brother or a sister. In accepting his past, Scott Mills also becomes subject to the humiliating and at times debilitating institutional racism of the Canadian state.

The stories of these two men are by no means unique. Their personal life stories illuminate a process in which industrial capitalism restructured kin-systems creating a social category "white" against which was posited a category "Indian." The dehumanizing and expropriating processes of colonial and capitalist development create the need and despite themselves open the space for the emergence of collective identities which may be class, ethnic, racial, or regional.

In British Columbia, despite attempts to build universalist working-class organizations, the dominant cleavages in the fishing industry have almost always been expressed in racial or ethnic terms (even in the context of labour organization itself). As the first step in shaking the beast of capital from our backs, focal, ethnic, or racial identities may be useful. Ultimately, however, such identities only serve to shackle us to the divisions created by capital and turn us away from the fundamental sameness of our different lives, cultures, and identities and our common experience as workers in a capitalist society.

References

Clement, Wallace

1986 The Struggle to Organize: Resistance in Canada's Fishery. Toronto: McClelland and Stewart.

Codere, Helen

1961 Fighting with Property: A Study of Kwakuitl Potlatching and Warfare, 1792-1930. American Ethnological Society Monograph #18, New York: J.J. Augustin.

Dyck, Noel

1986 Negotiating the Indian Problem. Culture 6(1): 31-41.

Fisher, Robin

1977 Contact and Conflict: Indian-European Relations in British Columbia, 1774-1890. Vancouver: University of British Columbia Press.

Garfield, Viola Edmundsom

1939 Tsimshian Clan and Society. University of Washington Publications in Anthropology 7(3):167-340.

Gladstone, Percy

1953 Native Indians and the Fishing Industry of British Columbia. Canadian Journal of Economics and Political Science 19(1).

Inglis, Joy and Harry Assu
  1969   Assu of Cape Mudge: Recollections of a Coastal Indian Chief. Vancouver: University of British Columbia Press.

Knight, Rolf
  1978   Indian's at Work: An Informal History of Native Indian Labour in British Columbia, 1858-1930. Vancouver: New Star Books.

McDonald, James A.
  1994   Social Change and the Creation of Underdevelopment: A Northwest Coast Case. American Ethnologist 21(1):152, 175.

Meggs, Geoff
  1991   Salmon: The Decline of the British Columbia Fishery. Vancouver/Toronto: Douglas & McIntyre.

Menzies, Charles Robert
  1994   Stories From Home: First Nations, Land Claims, and Euro-Canadians. American Ethnologist 21(4): 776-791.

Moore, Henrietta L.
  1988   Feminism and Anthropology. Cambridge: Polity Press.

Newell, Diane
  1993   Tangled Webs of History: Indians and the Law in Canada's Pacific Coast Fisheries. Toronto: University of Toronto Press.

Pinkerton, Evelyn
  1987   Competition Among B.C. Fish-Processing Firms. *In* Marchak et al., eds. Uncommon Property: The Fishing and Fish Processing Industries in British Columbia. Toronto: Methuen, pp. 66-91.

Sider, Gerald M.
  1993   Lumbee Indian Histories: Race, Ethnicity, and Indian Identity in the Southern States. Cambridge: Cambridge University Press.

Spradley, James and James Sewid
  1969   Guests Never Leave Hungry: The Autobiography of James Sewid, Kwakiutl Man. New Haven: Yale University Press.

Tennant, Paul
  1990   Aboriginal People and Politics: The Indian Land Question in British Columbia, 1849-1989. Vancouver: University of British Columbia Press.

Wolf, Eric
  1982   Europe and the People Without History. Berkeley: University of California Press.

HEMMED IN AND SHUT OUT
Urban Minority Kids, Consumption, and Social Inequality in New Haven, Connecticut[1]

Elizabeth Chin

The View from the 'Ville

One summer afternoon during a rainstorm, Natalia and Asia sat on Natalia's stoop and talked about Barbie. It was a sultry afternoon in the Newhallville neighbourhood of New Haven, Connecticut, the kind where the humid air hangs as wet and heavy as the rain itself. Often referred to as the "'Ville" by local kids, Newhallville is a neighbourhood whose population is overwhelmingly black, with many poor, and a reputation for suffering the gamut of inner-city ills. Characterized by multiple forms of isolation – geographic, social, economic, and commercial – the inner city is an "other" place intimately tied to the rest of the nation, and the rest of the globe. Kids like Natalia and Asia are aware of these connections, but cognizant as well that the complex and contradictory circumstances of their lives often leave them at a disadvantage.

Newhallville residents have access to the same TV programs, the same stores, and the same goods that most other Americans do, but their relationships to these consumer goods – and the process of consumption itself – is distinctive. Natalia and Asia's comments about Barbie keenly express these girls' own sense of where they are located in the world, and in relation to consumption:

1   This work was generously funded by dissertation grants from the Wenner-Gren Foundation, the National Science Foundation, and the Graduate School and University Center of the City University of New York. Mary Weismantel has, as always, given critical feedback in both senses of the word. The children and families among whom I worked in New Haven have been my mentors in all that I do. Their patience and kindness have been limitless and my debt to them is limitless as well.

ASIA: You never see a fat Barbie. You never see a pregnant Barbie. What about those things? They should make a Barbie that can have a baby.

NATALIA: Yeah . . . and make a fat Barbie. So when we play Barbie . . . you could be a fat Barbie.

ASIA: OK. What I was saying that Barbie . . . how can I say this? They make her like a stereotype. Barbie is a stereotype. When you think of Barbie you don't think of fat Barbie . . . you don't think of pregnant Barbie. You never, ever . . . think of an abused Barbie.

As Asia and Natalia were talking about Barbie, they were holding my tape recorder. "I would like to say that Barbie is dope," Natalia said, "But y'all probably don't know what that means so I will say that Barbie is *nice*!" A few minutes later, Asia had taken on an Oprah-like persona and was pretending to address an invisible, nation-wide television audience. "The streets . . . of Newhallville . . . next on the Asia show," she intoned with the same sort of dramatic, overblown mock solemnity pioneered on daytime talk shows.

These girls' dialogue reveals their awareness that this imaginary audience knows little about the character of Newhallville or the people who live there. Asia's stance is critical, playful, and ironic all at once. She knows that the Oprah audience is not interested in "the streets of Newhallville," as they are and how she experiences them, but rather they want to see and hear about "The STREETS . . . of NEWHALLVILLE." Likewise, Natalia recognizes that such audiences literally do not speak her language, and she roughly translates the richly evocative "dope" as the equivalent of the nearly image-free word "nice." The girls' ability to play with important consumer media – television, for instance – while on home turf is important, particularly because they did not play with these media in other settings, specifically the mall. Similarly, while at home they do not play with themes of sex and romance which in the neighbourhood are threatening, oppressive forces. However within the confines of the mall, their romantic flights of fancy are powerfully imagined and playfully pursued as they indulge in long boy-chasing episodes and richly imagined romantic fantasies.

The neighbourhood influences in specific ways the nature of the girls' engagement with the consumer sphere. The girls' overt and often discussed fear of rape made it evident that they feel vulnerable in Newhallville specifically because they are young and female. "Do you know why men rape little kids?" Tionna asked Natalia one afternoon. "Because they can't talk, they can't say anything." Natalia, after a moment's consideration, answered, "well they rape girls, and women, too." Newhallville children are hemmed in at home, interacting with a consumer culture that rarely acknowledges their existence. In their own neighbourhoods, girls did not use consumer goods as a medium for either romantic fantasy or playful exploration of sexual themes. Rather, Barbie was invoked when girls gave voice to their sense of sexual danger and to their profound awareness of being disenfranchised from mainstream Euro-American culture.

At the mall, Newhallville kids are shut out in various ways. Here, the discomfort and threat experienced by these girls emanates not from men, but rather from the stores and employees. And yet, the open, airy, and generally controlled space of the enclosed mall seems to allow the girls a sense of physical safety they do not experience in their own neighbourhood. It is this sense of safety, perhaps, that provides one impetus for their freewheeling romantic fantasies, and their extended boy-chasing escapades. This contrasts sharply with the tension and discomfort they generally feel when in stores or when shopping.

Newhallville children undertake consumption under the same circumstances that shape all other aspects of their lives: in the midst of wrenching economic change, rising social unrest, and in the continuing, and some would argue deepening, atmosphere of racism. Both New Haven's downtown mall and its troubled urban neighbourhoods are the direct and indirect result of decades of federally funded urban renewal projects undertaken by city administrations. The effect of policies shaping the economic, geographic, social, and commercial context of New Haven has not been neutral. As money has poured into a struggling downtown, Newhallville and other areas have had to deal with shrinking school budgets, poorly maintained roads, and public libraries that hardly ever opened their doors. A changing economy, too, has left both New Haven and Newhallville short on jobs for the semi-skilled and unskilled workers who once filled factories and workshops. New Haven embodies many of the conflicts presently experienced in cities and towns that were once happily expanding at the forefront of the industrial revolution, boosted by two world wars. Few companies in New Haven make anything any more; its primary industries are the production and dissemination of knowledge – taking place at Yale University – and health care, which takes place in the city's hospitals. Though growing, neither of these employers is prepared to provide replacement jobs for those formerly employed in industry. The result has been a dramatic and precipitous rise in the unemployed and poor, most of whom are minorities.

The blame for the city's condition has most often been laid at the feet of minority community members, and nowhere is this more clear than in the conflicts taking place over the rehabilitation of the New Haven mall. Malls, as places specializing in the simulation of gracious civic life, are not often meant to include those from all socioeconomic levels, ethnic groups, or subcultures. The New Haven mall is, ideally, a place from which Newhallville's children are absent. As a result, a variety of strategies for maintaining the mall's atmosphere impinge directly on the lives of children like those from Newhallville. These include preventing public transportation access; regulating shoppers' style of dress; regulating access of youth; playing music certain groups are thought to dislike; closely following and watching youthful and minority shoppers as they browse in stores. All of these strategies make Newhallville children's experiences in the mall unlike those of their better off or lighter-skinned peers.

The growing social science literature on consumption often points out that "we think we are free when our choices have in fact been consciously constructed for us. ... This is a dangerous illusion of freedom" (Tomlinson 1990:13). Some see malls – the consumer meccas of our time – as presenting this "dangerous illusion" with particular effectiveness (Williams 1982). For Newhallville children, however, these places – particularly when compared to shopping in their own neighbourhoods – actually do offer a great deal of choice, albeit choice that is at some level circumscribed and predetermined both by a corporate entity and capitalism at large. At the same time, such choice is, however, not to be confused with freedom. For these children (and their families) these stores offer often painful glimpses of what they might be able to get if they only had the money.

Based upon ethnographic research conducted among black and Hispanic ten-year-olds in the Newhallville neighbourhood of New Haven, this essay details the ways in which local, city-wide and national conditions in economy, geography, and social conditions set the scene for children's consumption practices and experiences.

New Haven

Connecticut has the nation's highest per capita income, but the impressive concentration of wealth in the state is rivaled by oppressive concentrations of poverty. Housing, education, jobs, and commercial districts are unequally distributed as well. These inequalities are starkly evident in New Haven.

Located eighty miles northeast of New York City on the shore of Long Island Sound, New Haven is a medium-sized city with 130,000 residents. It is the seventh poorest city of its size in the United States; for cities over 100,000, New Haven ranks first in the nation in infant mortality (Reguero 1994).[2] At the same time, New Haven is home to one of the nation's wealthiest and most elite educational institutions, Yale University. The city also possesses a bustling drug trade, a bankrupt shopping mall, a struggling downtown area, and deeply troubled public schools. Once a manufacturing-based town producing tires, beer, paper, apparel, and bagels, New Haven's population has shrunk by over 20,000 since its peak in the 1950s and the primary employment sector is today service-based.

Newhallville

With a reputation as one of the poorest and most troubled areas of the city, Newhallville's residents (91.7 percent of whom are minority) have a median household income in 1990 of $20,569; 26.6 percent of Newhallville residents live in poverty (U.S. Department of Commerce 1993).[3]

Sycamores and maples line the streets, their arching branches creating a tunnel-like effect. The two-and three-story wood frame clapboard houses and the occasional six-to ten-unit apartment building have small, grassy yards front and back where children play and where gardens of flowers or vegetables are planted. Newhallville has neither tenements nor housing projects. The poor live side by side with owners of homes and businesses; on occasion the poor are themselves owners of homes and businesses. After a property tax hike of about 40 percent in 1992 (the first step in a five-part tax increase due to raise payments a startling average of 238 percent), abandoned buildings – fallout from bankruptcies and the vagaries of absent landlords – have begun to multiply at an alarming rate and can be found on almost every block in the neighbourhood (62.6 percent of Newhallville housing units are rentals: United States Department of Commerce 1993). Boarded up, covered in graffiti, used as crack houses, these buildings were one sign in the early 1990s that the troubles in Newhallville were more than an undercurrent. Most blocks have also at least one empty lot filling with trash and discarded household appliances. Gunshots are a

---

2   In New Haven there are 185 infant deaths per 1,000 live births. There are some who argue the infant mortality rate in the city is inflated because Yale-New Haven Hospital has one of the nation's premiere neonatal units, and thus a higher concentration than normal of women with high-risk pregnancies and seriously ill infants. However, with one New Haven neighbourhood showing an infant mortality rate of 66.7 deaths per 1,000 live births [Reguero, 1994] there are strong indications that the city has deep problems in pre-natal and neonatal health.

3   In contrast, in 1960 the Newhallville poverty rate was 17.6 percent for all persons; Newhallville's ethnic mix was 18.2% white, 81.2% "Negro," and .6% other. Between 1960 and 1990, then, the poverty rate rose by half (51%), while the minority population increase was not commensurate, growing 12.9%. Newhallville's racial segregation does not appear to have a simple cause-and-effect relationship with the area's rapid rise in poverty.

common occurrence, street-dealing of drugs takes place at several well-known sites as well as many more clandestine ones. At night in Newhallville, police routinely stop cars driven by young, white men on the assumption that they have only entered the neighbourhood to buy drugs.

When Newhallville is referred to as a ghetto or inner-city neighbourhood, it is the large minority population, visible drug trade, deteriorating housing stock, and high poverty rate that are being indirectly referenced. Susan D. Greenbaum, writing about a similar neighbourhood in Kansas City, Kansas, cautions that "Ghetto is a monolithic concept, describing districts that may be ethnically uniform but which reflect a large degree of variability, both internally and among different cities. ...When folk categories like ghetto are reified and made respectable in the models and taxonomies of scholars and analysts, consequences and intentions become viciously intertwined" (Greenbaum 1993:140). If Newhallville, with its graceful trees and carefully painted frame houses does not appear to be a "typical" ghetto or inner-city community, it is because these terms assume a great deal, and like the term "underclass" are so poorly specified as to what, exactly, they refer, that they are nearly useless for the purposes of social science.

Avoiding the loaded terminology of "ghetto" or "inner city," I instead focus on characteristics that set Newhallville and neighbourhoods like it apart from the cities in which they are located. Among the most important of these elements are geographic, social, economic, and commercial isolation. These overlapping forms of isolation are not solely the result of an inward-turning community but one from which much of the rest of the city has turned away.

Geographic Isolation

Newhallville is a neighbourhood that most residents must leave in order to shop or work. Stepping over Newhallville borders is a charged activity, and many Newhallville residents – like the Sistah in "Free Your Mind" – do not feel welcome in other New Haven neighbourhoods, or in the city's downtown. These tensions and conflicts imbue most everyday activities with their peculiar flavour; the consumer lives of Newhallville children, under these circumstances, are similarly seasoned with these tensions and conflicts.

Newhallville's northern edge is at the border of the suburban town of Hamden. Where Hamden begins the streets abruptly become better paved, and a sleek junior high school atop a grassy hill overlooks Newhallville's increasingly decrepit Jackie Robinson Junior High. In contrast to Hamden's windowed, brick school, Jackie

Robinson is bunker-like and largely subterranean. Dominated by an orange color scheme, Jackie Robinson resembles nothing so much as a surreal prison. Much of this border area on the Hamden side is buffered by a sizable but inconvenient, uninviting, and underdeveloped park covering an area equal to about four or five city blocks.

To the east lies Prospect Street, which winds its way along the ridge of a hill separating Newhallville from the affluent Prospect Hill and East Rock neighbourhoods. Lined on both sides with old mansions of twenty or more rooms, Prospect Street is not a place that any Newhallville resident I knew ever approached on foot. One man referred to Prospect Street as the "DMZ," the demilitarized zone, a sort of dangerous and charged no-man's land to be avoided. The street itself is wide, an impression that is magnified by the expanses of lawn stretching out before houses set back well away from the street. In contrast to the stoops and front porches in Newhallville where people sit, observe the action, or keep tabs on their children, Prospect Street marks the transition into neighbourhoods where people stay indoors or in backyards, minding their own business.

On Newhallville's southern edge, the site of the Winchester Repeating Arms plant occupies a space equivalent to perhaps half a dozen square blocks, creating a buffer – or bulwark – between Newhallville and the city beyond. Now only partially occupied by gun production facilities, the bulk of the former factory has been torn down or rehabbed for other uses. The largest project has been Science Park, a business development whose purpose was to attract scientific research and development companies. In the process of transforming the former site of the Winchester Repeating Arms factory into Science Park, a portion of Winchester Avenue – a main neighbourhood thoroughfare – was closed to the public. Gates manned by twenty-four-hour guards now stand at corners that had once been bus stops. The message is clear: Newhallville residents literally have been shut out of their own neighbourhood. That this has taken place on a site that once was the area's main employer has only added insult to injury.

Processes hemming in Newhallville residents work in reverse downtown: in the city's center people like those living in Newhallville are shut out. During the early 1990s the Yale campus, like the Winchester site, became progressively more enclosed by walls, gates, and guarded entrances. While town-gown relations have long been problematic, such visible efforts to shut residents out of the campus noticeable exacerbated tensions. The permanent closing of a block of Wall Street in the downtown area of the campus – for which Yale compensated the city with a one-time payment – fueled suspicions of many minority residents that city hall and the University are in cahoots to fence them out. These suspicions took shape in a rumour that the city and Yale have together cooked up a plan to up a plan to cut off water and electricity to selected parts of the city should there ever be a repeat of the riots in the black community that took place in 1967. As one young man said, "They'll starve us out!"

Social Isolation

Newhallville receives few visitors – unless they are from nearby Dixwell, another poor neighbourhood, or have relatives there. Those outsiders who do regularly come are mostly educators, police officers, health care workers, social science and medical students. Most are white and middle-class, and a number of them are uniformed, and so their status as outsiders is visible and underscored in multiple ways – not the least of which is that most are there to mend or circumvent social problems. This visibility is often though not always characterized by tension. In particular, teachers at the elementary school (many of whom are black) are well-loved and respected. The city's police chief, Nick Pastore, can often be found in front of the Newhallville conununity police station – early in the morning, midday, and late at night, clad in a white shirt and tie, talking with neighbourhood kids, teenagers and adults, and dispensing his signature hug to nearly everyone who comes within his reach.

Although New Haven's population is fifty-one percent minority, the city's diversity has not resulted in an integrated residential sector: 11 of New Haven's 28 census tracts had minority populations of 60 percent or more in 1990 (United States Department of Commerce 1993). With a long-standing presence in New Haven that stretches back nearly to the colonial period, the African-American population in New Haven grew significantly during these postwar boom years. Between 1950 and 1960 that population more than doubled from 9,600 to 23,000 (Minerbrook 1992:37). More recently, immigrants from Central America and the Caribbean have increased the city's minority population. These immigrants have not settled in Newhallville, however, but in other neighbourhoods such as "the Hill," or in nearby Fair Haven.

Residential segregation, already well under way in the first half of the 20th century, was given a big boost in the years during which New Haven undertook extensive urban redevelopment. The social isolation of neighbourhoods such as Newhallville may be seen as being primarily a product of urban redevelopment, not the result of social factors internal to the Newhallville community. Getting in on the bottom floor of the nation's urban revitalization efforts, New Haven emerged as the nation's model "model city" by the time the Great Society years were in full swing (Fainstein 1974).

From the late 1950s through the early 1970s, over half a billion federal dollars funded urban redevelopment projects. Urban revitalization ostensibly sought to wipe out blight but many so-called improvements had a debilitating impact on the black community. Urban renewal projects eventually displaced almost forty percent of New Haven's black population, levelling long-standing communities of houses and home owners to relocate residents in housing projects which were owned and administrated by city and federal agencies. Between 1950 and 1970 about 10,000 units of housing were destroyed (Minerbrook 1992); equivalent replacement housing never materialized, and most new units were intended for middle-class and elderly residents. New Haven's residential segregation, and hence its social isolation, is hardly the result of such processes as individual preference; rather, it can be seen as the not wholly surprising outcome of programmatic urban restructuring undertaken by successive New Haven political administrations and city agencies in conjunction with Federal programs.

Economic Isolation

The character and population of Newhallville has changed dramatically in forty years. From the time that the neighbourhood's main employer was the carriage factory owned by George T. Newhall until the 1950s, the area had been occupied primarily by German and Irish and finally Italian immigrants of the working class. Then soon after the end of World War II, throughout New Haven, large industrial employers began downsizing and relocating. The changing fortunes of the Winchester Repeating Arms plant capture the upheavals that have faced New Haven and Newhallville residents in the past fifty years. From the turn of the century until the 1950s, Winchester was a major employer in New Haven and the focal center of Newhallville. During the years around World War II, Winchester employed 12,000 people, many of them from Newhallville. By the 1970s changing employment opportunities left a bleak vista. Winchester's roster, for example, had dropped over forty percent to 7,000 workers. By the 1990s, the entire city of New Haven had just over 7,000 manufacturing jobs and only 475 people worked at Winchester in 1992.

Like many other places nationwide, New Haven has made the transition from a manufacturing-based economy to one where service industries provide the lion's share of jobs. Today New Haven's largest employers are Yale University and the Yale-New Haven Hospital, together accounting for 14,979 jobs (New Haven Downtown Council 1992). These jobs are, on the whole, not only less plentiful than their manufacturing counterparts once were; they are less secure, offer fewer benefits, lower pay, and often require higher degrees of literacy or special technical skills that necessitate secondary or vocational education. Given that the cumulative dropout rate for New Haven high schools is probably near forty percent,[4] there is a great probability that public school students, at least, are unlikely to acquire the needed skills and education to secure available jobs.

Employment is a primary problem in Newhallville. Efforts to develop unused portions of the Winchester plant into a business park have yielded little. Only a small portion of the old factory had been refurbished as a development for science-based businesses and renamed "Science Park." Most of this newly developed space remained unoccupied. The irony of the situation has only been intensified by one of the most visible occupants of Science Park, the New Haven Family Alliance, a non-profit organization devoted to helping dysfunctional families and troubled youth. Neighbourhood residents must ask security guards for permission to enter the former site of their (or their parents') employment in order to visit an organization whose purpose is to help families deal with stress and behaviours brought on by their poverty and underemployment.

Commercial Isolation

In the 1950s, the area had developed a varied and lively commercial sphere and was home to a dry cleaners, at least two drug stores, one corporate supermarket and several small-to-medium sized groceries, a butcher, several luncheonettes, two laundromats, one (and possibly more) dentists' and doctors' offices, hardware stores, and auto repair shops. In addition, according to long-time residents, the neighbourhood housed a dairy plant, the Winchester plant, a pharmaceutical distribution company, and a popcorn supply house.

Not only constituent elements of the consumer setting, these last establishments were large-scale employers of neighbourhood residents. Many local businesses, moreover, provided crucial services – particularly medical care. Today, the only neighbourhood medical care available is from the MotherCare van, a mobile facility parked in front of the local elementary school every Thursday.[5]

A series of incidents related to police clashes with local Black Panther leaders and the riots in 1967 in which the federal government deployed the National Guard

---

4   Official figures are hard to obtain here. This figure was quoted to me by the head of the citywide PTA. I was also told by several school administrators that significant numbers of drop outs occur in the junior high school years. High school drop out rates, then, fail to account for those students who have dropped out before starting high school.

5   Funded and operated by the local Catholic hospital, the MotherCare van provides prenatal, pediatric, and general health care, but does not provide services or information related to birth control or abortion.

drove some white business owners out of the neighbourhood; other businesses were destroyed in the burning and looting that took place. Jackson Rollins, who took me on two walking tours of his childhood neighbourhood, remembers the doctor, dentist, hardware store, and pharmacy all to have been white-owned. The black-owned enterprises that came in afterward did not replace these businesses in kind: as can be seen today, they are typically small groceries, barbershops, liquor stores, and bars. Further, as Winchester and other large employers closed, businesses (such as lunch counters) which catered to factory workers foundered. Finally, an urban revitalization plan – undertaken with limited community support according to some residents – razed a large stretch of shops in preparation for a modem, new shopping strip. This new commercial center was never built.

The main places that Newhallville children frequent are corner stores, such as Rabbit's grocery, where the owner dispenses as much advice as he does change. These stores are small, and typically carry perhaps five hundred different items, compared to the 25,000 items a large supermarket is likely to stock. Kids buy chips, gum, candy, and drinks before and after school, or stop in to play video games. In comparison to large supermarkets, small markets like Rabbit's offer little choice and high prices to boot. It is difficult for a family which does not own or have access to a car to provide nourishing meals if shopping only in the neighbourhood, but the nearest supermarkets are nearly two miles away.

The Mall

If kids – or their families – want any item such as clothing, housewares, or toys, they must go downtown to the mall, or drive even further to local suburban shopping areas. Going to the mall is at once exciting and frustrating for kids from Newhallville, who are often treated with suspicion. Children's experiences at the mall illustrate the ways in which consumption is entered into and experienced as a realm of inequality – one in which other forms of inequality come into play.

Late in April of 1992, it was announced that Macy's, the New Haven mall's anchor store, would close in June. Near bankruptcy, the mall was a sinking ship. On April 1 a *New Haven Register* headline read, "White Person Slips, Falls at Mall; Black Teenager Being Sought." It turned out the headline was an April Fool's day joke published by the *New Haven*, a local weekly tabloid that emulates the *Village Voice*. The headline condensed several prickly issues New Haven residents were mulling over: the widely held perception that the local newspaper is less than evenhanded in how it reports on the black community; that the mall is an unsafe place for white shoppers; and that African-American kids are the reason why whites feel uncomfortable there. This tension between the middle class, predominantly white, and often suburban population and the poorer and darker New Haven residents is one that typifies malls throughout the country, particularly those located near urban areas (Everett 1994). Rather than braving the city, the logic went, suburban shoppers stayed closer to home, shopping at malls in the nearby towns of Milford and Hamden where the "inner-city ills" to which Everett alludes above are at least minimized.

Malls in Connecticut, including New Haven, have taken steps to reduce the presence of minority youth. After a protracted legal battle, one Connecticut mall, Trumbull Shopping Park, gained the right to ban public transit from making stops on its property on Friday and Saturday nights. The owners' express reason for making this decision was security problems arising from teenagers – most of whom were minority youth from Bridgeport. New Haven had employed a similar strategy, moving bus stops from directly in front of the mall to relocate them across the street on the town green. This move considerably increased discomfort for bus riders. The original bus stops, located in front of the mall, were placed on a covered walkway open to the street that provided at least some protection from rain and snow. Across the way on the green, two rather small bus shelters hardly provide the same amount of protection from harsh weather conditions.

Some malls have gone so far as to monitor kids' dress, and the Sunrise Mall in Corpus Christi, Texas, even instituted a policy banning backward-facing baseball caps (*New York Times* 1/9/95). As a result, fashion trends among poor and minority youth are branded as signaling trouble and are likely to be prohibited from the mall. Practices such as dressing alike – common among many minority youth and not just gangs – are increasingly likely to get kids ejected from malls on the grounds that dressing alike is in itself a marker of gang affiliation. This trend is significantly more troubling than the old "No shirt, no shoes, no service" policies that were at least usually clearly posted.

In most cases policies limiting kids' access to malls, their appearance, or their behaviour have been spurred by violent incidents involving guns, and, in two cases, fatal shootings. Ironically, these much-feared kids often say themselves that they go to the mall in order to be safe. In New Haven, the neighbourhoods these kids come from – Newhallville, The Hill, Dixwell – are widely held by residents and outsiders alike to be unpredictably dangerous.

The owners of the seventy shops in the Chapel Square Mall considered for a time a proposal to limit the hours during which unaccompanied young people could be on the premises. When word of the proposal reached the public, it was widely criticized as racist. The conflict was typical of those cropping up around the country on the nature of mall spaces: are they public or private? How do you define "security"? If the spaces were deemed public, shop owners hardly had the legal right to bar access to kids, although the management company that runs New Haven's mall already has an official policy of keeping school-age shoppers out of the mall during school hours. If the spaces were private, mall owners could legally be held accountable for thefts, robberies, and injuries suffered by visitors.

Regardless of the reasons for which consumers who are older, more affluent, or lighter-skinned have abandoned Chapel Square, youth and teens (mostly minority) now constitute the mall's most important market (*New York Times* 11/23/93). Shop owners have had to develop subtle means of discouraging young people from spending too much time in the mall's public spaces, while enticing them to continue to spend their money in its commercial venues. These strategies include an increasingly visible uniformed security force and the use of piped music featuring genres thought to be unappealing to undesirable youth. In a variation of what Russell Baker (*New York Times* 7/23/92) jokingly called "the Beethoven Defense," I found on one visit to the New Haven mall the building's hidden speakers filling the space with songs by Frank Sinatra.

Though the relatively large proportion of black shoppers in the New Haven mall might have had something to do with its economic decline, there nevertheless seem to be other factors at work. In comparison to larger, newer, and more architecturally and visually spectacular malls, the New Haven mall – which was built in the 1960s – is rundown, offers little variety, and in contradiction of a basic mall dictum the parking is not even free. Currently the mall houses no outlets of prominent chains such as Gap, Express, Banana Republic, Pottery Barn, Crate & Barrel; instead, discount enterprises – Sam's Dollar Store, and Payless Shoes, for example – are in the majority.

Development of nearby areas has encouraged the movement of moneyed shoppers away from the mall. A prominent local development company, Schiavone, has considerably perked up the Upper Chapel Street area that is located two blocks above the mall and directly across from part of the Yale Campus. This newly-renovated stretch of shops and restaurants is now distinctly upscale, housing downtown's priciest venues. Further up, the rundown Broadway area is currently being rehabbed with a $7.5 million federal grant and a: $1.9 million contribution from Yale siphoning off whatever upscale business remains downtown and relocating it closer to the Yale campus.

Lower Chapel, which once housed a large Kresge's store (Kresge's is the predecessor of K-Mart), is now home to discount stores and jewelry shops. Nearly all those shopping on Lower Chapel are black and Hispanic; while shoppers on Upper Chapel and Broadway are racially and ethnically diverse, few are poor or working-class. As one person, who had grown up in Dixwell, which borders the Broadway shopping area, said "We used to go down there to look at the people walking funny!" This remark was accompanied by a raucous imitation of the stiff, uptight walk of the middle class, whites, or fearful Yale students.

In a city already starkly segregated in its residential areas, downtown is now headed toward a similar segregation. Lower and Upper Chapel streets house shopping areas that cater to starkly different clientele. The mall physically occupies the middle ground between the two, and though perceived to be used by an ever-poorer and darker population, people who go there remain relatively diverse in both race and social and economic level, especially when compared to the territories on either side. As the physical and perceptual middle ground downtown, the mall is a conflicted site. Many shopkeepers are caught between trying to appeal to all economic levels of customers while others have attempted to capitalize upon the mall's changing demographic mix and have opened stores carrying hip-hop fashions, African folklore and artisanry, or Afro-centric merchandise.

The Chapel Square mall is not unusual in its attempts to maintain a profile as a safe, communal space that exists in distinct opposition to the chaotic, violent city beyond. Such consumer community-building amounts to the proffering of togetherness through shopping. This effort is most evident in the yearly Christmas spree of conviviality and community events sponsored by the mall.

Halloween has more recently emerged as a time when the mall is offered as a healthy alternative to the New Haven streets and all its dangers. This effort is supported not only by its own publicity efforts but by institutions such as the public schools. Since the early 1990s, mall shopkeepers have distributed candy and Halloween balloons to hordes of costumed kids who trick-or-treat their way around the two-story concourse on a weekend near the 31st of October. Significantly, this event is designed to appeal to young children and their families, segments of the population mall management finds amenable, not problematic older children and teens. During my fieldwork, the principal of the Lincoln school sent a note to each child's family that encouraged caretakers not to allow their children to trick-or-treat door to door, but instead advised them either to take children only to family members' homes, or to go trick-or-treating at the mall. While in this scary world you cannot be sure that your neighbours will not insert razor blades into the apples they put in your child's goodie bag, you can trust that local store owners are not so perverse as to harm their customers or their families.

Community, in this situation, is not based on the kinds of mutual obligation and civic commitment embodied in the notion of neighbourliness, because you cannot trust those you know. Trick-or-treating is safer amidst the relative anonymity of the mall, where shopkeepers know better than to bite the hand that feeds them. While refraining from the bite, shopkeepers do bark, and it is at their young customers that they bark most often.

Newhallville Girls Go to the Mall

From the time they are very small, Newhallville children accompany their families, whether parents or older siblings and cousins, on downtown shopping excursions. When children – especially girls – are about ten years old, many of their families begin allowing them to go downtown without the accompaniment of their elders. Among the children from the main study group, girls go downtown alone more often than do boys, who spend much of their unsupervised time riding bikes around the neighbourhood – or farther afield.

For these girls, going to the mall without adults is often a thrilling experience, and one that allows them to be playful in ways that are impossible at home and in the neighbourhood. Despite widespread feelings in New Haven that the mall is not a particularly safe or comfortable space to be, the statements and behaviour of Newhallville children indicate that for them, the mall offers freedoms unavailable elsewhere, while also imposing particular forms of restraint.

Spatial Freedom

As mentioned earlier, some kids go to the mall because they feel safer there than they do on the street. "Kids come here to stay out of trouble and to shop," said sixteen-year-old Cherie Lee in an interview with the *New York Times* (11/23/93). Though none of the kids I knew stated this feeling quite so directly, I was struck by the changes in their demeanor when we went to the mall. Some of these changes had more to do with the social setting than with the spaces or architecture of the mall itself. While the spatial and social aspects of Newhallville kids' mall experiences are examined here separately, these are ultimately mutually determining.

Malls are often compared to theme parks such as Disneyland in part because like theme parks, malls feature controlled, utopian, yet carnival atmospheres. Several recent megamalls, such as the Mall of America in Minnesota or West Edmonton Mall in Canada (with 5.2 million square feet) actually contain theme parks, further eliding the two forms that are at once architectural, social, and economic. Tionna, Natalia, and Asia, when they went to the mall often used its spaces as their own kind of personal amusement center, going down the up escalators, and up the down ones, running through public spaces loudly laughing and shouting, and tailing cute boys like easy-to-spot, giggly spies. Before Macy's had closed, the second-floor breezeway connecting the mall to the department store was a glass-encased tunnel through which they could run, gallop, shuffle, or tumble. Macy's itself was a kind of playground, with its three floors, numerous escalators, and accessible displays of electronics, jewelry, and makeup. Excerpts of field notes from a shopping expedition taken shortly before Christmas in 1992 detail some of the typical activities in which kids engaged when visiting the mall:

Asia and Natalia lean over the second floor railing throwing pennies into the fountain below on the mall's main floor. Bunches of poinsettia plants are set high upon wire pillars that rise up out of the fountain and the brilliant red flowers seem to float in the air. By the edge of the fountain is a cart whose proprietors are selling religious clocks and metal, laser-etched images of saints and reproductions of the Last Supper. Asia and Natalia decide to try to throw a coin down on top of someone's head. They drop some pennies down. The coins miss the unsuspecting person, who is minding the cart with the Last Supper reproductions. The girls come running up to me, jumping, hopping, vibrating with the excitement and danger of what they have done. Then they spot some cute boys and take off in close pursuit. I take off after them.

They have lost the boys and decide to look for them in the Macy's game section one floor up. They go up there, pretending to shop, looking at electronic typewriters. The boys are not there. After a few minutes of playing and fiddling with electronic displays, Natalia says, "Now we got to go boy huntin' again." As we are walking, Asia says, "Miss Chin looks hype. All she got to do is lose the bags." Natalia, however, announces, "Miss Chin is bad luck." Meaning it's my fault they lost the boys. We are by the escalator and the girls consider going downstairs. "That's where the perfume is," Natalia says. We go up to the third floor again. No boys. "Miss Chin, you're making us lose men," Natalia wails. We go all the way to the first floor and the girls stop at the Clinique counter for a few minutes, playing with the facial "computer" there. We head back upstairs again, on an escalator, and on the way the girls place coins on the moving rubber rail, calling to me and saying, "We gave the coins a ride!"

In pursuing the boys the thrill is in the chase itself. Exploring different departments in Macy's, playing with electronic typewriters and children's toys, riding the escalators, fiddling with cosmetics displays are fun and exciting for these kids. These activities would be fun for any kids, but what was absent from the surface, at least, of these children's playful meandering, was any engagement with most spaces as consumers with money to spend. They played with the typewriters just to play with them, not so that they could think about buying them or even wish that they could have one of their own. The escalators were by far the most exciting and fascinating element, aside from a certain pleasure they seemed to take in knowing they were on the verge of wildness – all the roaming up and down and up and down again – and yet unlikely to suffer any painful consequences.

This was their mall: a large, open, interesting, exciting space, full of cute boys and girls and dotted with inconvenient security guards and disapproving grownups; lined with stores containing fascinating merchandise; punctuated by escalators that lifted them to the mysteries above or lowered them to the unknown below. They were not there only or even primarily to shop, but to explore, to go "boy huntin'" as Natalia said, and to generate a safe, yet thrilling, excitement. This is not the sort of use for which Macy's or the mall were designed or perhaps intended; like the amusement park, Macy's and the mall presented the kids with a closely monitored – and hence relatively safe – space.

Social Freedom

Being at the mall does not place kids in a field of unadulterated freedom, but it does allow some pressures and problems to recede from the forefront of their experiences. Tionna, Natalia, and Asia can revel in being girls while at the mall. At home, they worry that men might be after them; in the mall, they chase boys as if every day were Sadie Hawkins day. The following are portions of an interaction that took place in the mall's food court:

> Asia spies a boy she knows. With ten-year-old bravado, Natalia says that she's going to get up and go over to them. Asia tells her to go ahead. Overcome with the idea, Natalia suddenly decides she can't possibly do it. Asia gets up and goes over to the boys, tells one of them that Natalia likes him. Natalia squirms, moans, giggles, slides under the table and, emerging again, tries to bury herself inside her coat. Asia comes back. I drink my soda and they eat, glancing back at the boys who are sometimes looking our way. The taller boy comes over and says to Natalia that the other boy wants her to go over there. Now she's really dying. She's saying she's too shy and she can't talk to them.

The freedom might appear, from an adult point of view to be very childlike, even though much of it focuses on boy-girl interactions of a romantic nature. However, the girls, at least, think of these mall outings as a way to begin to explore growing up, not being kids. Tionna explained that at the mall "We try not to act like kids. When we're here, at home, then we act like kids, we play, we play with our dolls." Being able to explore the city and the mall on their own is thus a mark of maturity – one intrinsically opposed to the vulnerability of childhood and playing with dolls at home. Children often yearn to be grown-up for a whole host of reasons. For Tionna, Natalia, and Asia, one of these might be that feeling of freedom and safety they receive when roaming downtown.

Constraints

Minority youth are well aware that they are at best only temporarily welcome – and then only under certain circumstances – in most mall spaces, and that they are almost if not literally unwelcome in others. The loud and often disruptive behaviour of Newhallville kids in the mall can be seen in part as an assertion of their right not only to be where they are, but to be in the world.

The most obvious way that kids are made to feel self-conscious is when store employees or owners pointedly watch or follow them as they move through stores. Children are extremely sensitive to this. Asia, when preparing to enter Claire's, an inexpensive accessory store, recounted a recent experience in which she imagines being able to one-up a salesclerk whom she feels had mocked her on an earlier occasion because she was short of money:

> "Last time I was in there the lady was laughing because I didn't have enough money. The other day I went in and I bought all this stuff and the lady said, 'that will be forty dollars.' I pulled out a fifty dollar bill and said, 'Here.'" Asia demonstrated, and the look on her face was both self-satisfied and challenging. "I swear I was about to say 'keep the change' until my grandmother came up," she said.

Asia's story captures the pressures many Newhallville kids face in having to assert their right to be in the mall by demonstrating their ability to buy. In Asia's story, when she is at first unable to pay for what she wants, she is sure that the saleslady is laughing at her. The pleasure she took later in being able to present this woman with a fifty dollar bill was palpable, as was her frustration in not being able to add insult to injury by imperiously directing the woman to keep the change.

These kinds of interactions – where black shoppers are assumed to be unable to make purchases, where they are steered toward inferior merchandise, or where they are poorly treated as if giving them attention is a waste of time – are recounted often by young and old alike. These kinds of problems are one reason, for instance, why many Newhallville residents dress up when going downtown to shop: it is an effort to appear respectable to store personnel, and so to be treated with attention and respect.

Regardless of the impressions kids want to create, money is often an issue for them. Walking through Macy's one afternoon, Asia spotted an outfit she thought was "cute." After looking at the price tag, however, she said "Once you see the price of clothes it's not cute any more. It's expensive." Kid's experience of desire was circumscribed by their own sense of what was a good price for something – and, I suspect, by their keen knowledge of the limited nature of their own and their family's finances.

Two mothers told me why it is so important to rein in children's desires, and to require them to suppress those desires:

> "If you get them used to having all this stuff, when they get older and you say no, they get real upset," Diana said, explaining why she is so adamant now about saying "when I say no it means no," to the kids. "I don't promise them things," she said. "I say, 'we'll see.'" "What do you mean when you say they get upset?" I asked. "Well," said Yvonne, "if you buy them all these expensive things when they're little, they still expect you to buy it when they're older. My mother raised seven children alone and she worked three jobs. She always got us the best of everything. She went to the best stores, we always had nice clothes. Now I still get mad when I can't have things. I can act like a little kid, and I say 'I want that!'"

More than once I came across children in Newhallville with tear-stained faces, after they had been punished for being "bad" in the store, which usually meant asking one time too many for something. By the time kids are nine or ten, they seem to know better than to ask or pester. In the course of the research I took over twenty-five separate shopping trips with children, yet I only heard them say "I want that" once or twice. Only one child directly asked me to purchase anything. He later explained to me that he was purposely testing me and announced, "You weak!" Several refused my offers to buy them small things, such as a soda or ice cream cone, saying "I don't want to spend up all your money, Miss Chin!"

Conclusion

In the summer of 1992, music from the debut album of the 90s girl group En Vogue was a hit nationwide in the United States. All over Newhallville the song floated out of open windows, or erupted from the bass-heavy speakers of passing cars. Kids enthusiastically belted out words to one of the album's songs, "Free Your Mind":

> So I'm a sistah
> Buy things with cash
> That really doesn't mean that all my credit is bad
> So why dispute me and waste my time
> Because you think that the price is too high for me
> I can't look without being watched
> You rang my buy before I made up my mind
> Oh now attitude why even bother
> I can't change your mind you can't change my color

In a song that criticizes and questions racism and sexism, an entire verse is dedicated to the experience of consumption. This song resonated strongly among Newhallville's children: for them – as for many African Americans – shopping is a consumer activity fraught with conflict and contradiction. "Free Your Mind" high-lights a number of issues that Newhallville kids often confront: the assumptions made by salespeople that a "sistah" who pays with cash also has bad credit (and is therefore poor); of being watched while shopping (because they are potential shoplifters); of being treated with a lack of respect and politeness (because they are poor, potential shoplifters, and black). The final line in the verse pinpoints the problem as one of racism: "I can't change your mind, you can't change my color."

Popular stereotypes of African Americans often hinge on what is perceived to be their pathological involvement with consumption. From the image of the welfare queen – stereotypically an unwed teenage mother who has dropped out of school to live off the state while buying Nike sneakers for herself – to the gold-draped and logo-clad drug dealer who feels no remorse at committing random violence in the pursuit of territory or profits or debts, black consumers are viewed as being what have been described as "a nation of thieves" (Austin 1994). The En Vogue song, however, illuminates another point of view and instead describes the frustration, anger, and humiliation often felt by black shoppers whether at the supermarket or Saks Fifth Avenue.

Consumption is a complex process that involves not just shopping and buying but also thinking about, wishing for, and using commodities in a variety of settings and for a variety of purposes. Because consumption is fundamentally social, it is at once a sphere of inequality on its own and a medium through which other forms of inequality are perpetuated. As with other forms of structural inequality – such as class, race, and gender – the mechanisms perpetuating inequalities in the consumer sphere are subtly enforced in and through mundane activities: watching television, shopping, reading, playing. The children who are the subject of this work witness and experience themselves as situated in race, class, gender, and age as they see ads for things they know they cannot possess, as they are closely monitored when browsing in stores, as they play with toys whose fantasy lives they reject.

In Asia's critique of Barbie, she observes that there is no fat Barbie, no abused Barbie, a comment that directly addresses the doll's inability to speak to some of the central concerns of Asia's own life. In the neighbourhood, where protecting oneself from sexual danger is part of the daily routine, it is striking that Asia does not even enter a playful mode when she discusses this issue as it relates to a toy. The incident did, however, contain some powerful aspects of playfulness – these related not to Barbie, but to consumer media themselves such as television, the narrative form of the talk show, and the consuming public. The clear and critical voice and eye that Asia applies to her view of Barbie while on a Newhallville stoop becomes a little shakier at the mall, when she cannot confront a store clerk who she believes has humiliated her, with the same directness. While she wants to humiliate the woman in return, she cannot while actually at the mall. She is able to recover some of her bravado as she relates the story when back in her own neighbourhood, at a safe distance from the mall itself and the constraints it places upon her.

Surprisingly little research deals with the consumer lives of children and even less has directly addressed consumption in a nonwhite, nonmiddle-class setting (Honeycutt 1975 is one exception). This attention gap arises in part because the notion of the poor consumer is an apparent oxymoron: how can one be engaged with consumption without the means to consume? The common assumption is that those without economic resources who do consume do so dysfunctionally; poor consumers who are also black and young are portrayed not as being just dysfunctional but as being pathological in their patterns of consumption.

In a growing literary genre that seeks to portray life on the mean streets of big cities like Chicago, Los Angeles, and New York, out-of-control consumption is continually evoked to provide garish accent to descriptions of the grinding routine of living life in deep poverty. Liberal accounts such as *On the Edge* (Nightingale 1993) take the position that the pathology is not the fault, really, of any given individual, but is due to a faulty social system and the evils of consumption itself; conservative treatments of the issue see nothing much wrong with consumerism but rather bemoan the loss of family values, morals, and a lack of ability to delay gratification (Wilson 1987). My stance jibes with neither of these points of view. Consumption is much too pervasive to reject or wish away, and the issues presented by looking at consumption in communities like Newhallville must be understood not only as acts of individuals but as acts that also take place in a particular set of circumstances. What Newhallville kids do as they shop, try to earn money, or play with toys reflects, among other things, the fearsome struggles in which they must daily engage as they negotiate territories of race, class, gender, and age.

References

Austin, Regina
  1994   "A Nation of Thieves": Consumption, Commerce, and the Black Public
          Sphere. Public Culture 7(1):225-248.
City of New Haven
  1982   Inside New Haven's Neighborhoods: A Guide to the City of New Haven.
          New Haven: New Haven Colony Historical Society.
Commission, City of New Haven Blue Ribbon
  1990   Final Report of the Blue Ribbon Commission Appointed by Mayor John
          C. Daniels. City of New Haven, 1990.
Everett, Peter S.
  1994   Violence Comes to the Mall. Trial 30:62-65. Fainstein, Norman 1. and Susan
          S. Fainstein 1974 Urban Political Movements: The Search for Power by
          Minority Groups in American Cities. Englewood Cliffs: Prentice-Hall, Inc.
Greenbaum, Susan D.
  1993   Housing Abandonment in Inner-City Black Neighbourhoods: A Case Study
          of the Effects of the Dual Housing Market. *In* The Cultural Meaning of
          Urban Space. Robert Rotenberg and Gary McDonogh, eds. pp. 139-156.
          Westport: Bergin and Garvey.
Honeycutt, Andrew
  1975   An Ethnographic Study of Low Income Consumer Behavior. Unpublished
          DBS Dissertation, Harvard University.
Minerbrook, Scott
  1992   Why A City Alone Cannot Save Itself: The Story of New Haven Shows How
          Big Social and Economic Forces Overwhelm Local Leaders. U.S. News and
          World Report, November 9, 1992:36-40.

New Haven Downtown Council
  1992   Major Employers in New Haven County. New Haven Downtown Council,
          1992.

Nightingale, Carl
  1993   On the Edge: A History of Poor Black Children and their American Dreams.
          New York: Basic Books.

Reguero, Wilfred and Marilyn Crane
  1994   Project MotherCare: One Hospital's Response to the High Perinatal Death
          Rate in New Haven, CT. Public Health Reports 109(5):647-652.

Sorkin, Michael, ed.
  1992   Variations on a Theme Park: The New American City and the End of Public
          Space. New York: Farrar, Straus and Giroux.

Tomlinson, Alan
  1990   Introduction: Consumer Culture and the Aura of the Commodity. *In*
          Consumption, Identity, and Style: Marketing, Meanings and the Packaging
          of Pleasure. Alan Tomlinson, ed. Pp. 1-40. London and New York: Routledge.

U.S. Department of Commerce
  1993   Detailed Housing Characteristics: Connecticut. Government Printing Office,
          1993.

Williams, Rosalind H.
  1982   Dream Worlds: Mass Consumption in Late Nineteenth-Century France.
          Berkeley: University of California Press.

Wilson, William Julius
  1987   The Truly Disadvantaged: The Inner City, the Underclass, and Public Policy.
          Chicago: University of Chicago Press.

AIDS Rumours, Vulnerability, and the Banana Wars: A View From Dominica

Deidre Rose

Introduction

On September 22 2009 I received a "Cause Announcement" from the First Nations and Aboriginal Rights Group via Facebook. The missive informed readers that many people in the village of Ahousaht, British Columbia had been vaccinated against the H1N1 influenza and within the week over one hundred members of the community had fallen sick. The author stated that, "On the face of things, it appears that seasonal flu vaccinations and/or antiviral medications are causing a sickness that is being deliberately aimed at aboriginal people across Canada." The notice continued by citing historical precedents – this had happened before – as evidence for its strong claim. The mainstream media was quick to dismiss the claims as "unfounded" and based on "conspiracy theory" and "rumour." The case reminded me of the AIDS rumours that had been circulating in Dominica during the time of my fieldwork, and prompted me to revisit the ethnographic material collected then. In what follows, I intend to take seriously these rumours, not as statements of metaphysical truth, but as a kind of situated knowledge or counter-epistemology that can tell us something about the connections between experiences of colonial exploitation, slavery, racism, current economic globalization, the impact of economic crisis on health, and local reactions to HIV/AIDS and other pandemic intervention strategies.

Public health programs have done enormous good, but have also been met with skepticism. As the case of Ahousaht demonstrates, this skepticism may take the form of rumours about the motives of the intervention. Amy Kaler (2009) has written a summary article focusing on the recurrent theme of sterility rumours and vaccination programs. Using reports of sterility rumours from public health interventions in Africa, Kaler argues that "these rumours are more than simply stories which are not true. The widespread rumour of sterility is a way of articulating broadly shared understandings about reproductive bodies, collective survival, and global asymmetries of power" (Kaler 2009:1719). Kaler introduces the concept of "counter-epistemic convergence" to understand sterility rumours. Charles Briggs and Clara Mantini-Briggs (2003) have written a stunning analysis of Warao narratives and counter-narratives surrounding the outbreak of cholera in Venezuela and the tragic death of hundreds of Warao children, women, and men. They point out that public interventions that adopt "cultural reasoning" or any strategies that blame people with little social, economic, or political power do not help to prevent illness. AIDS prevention programs that focus on cultural or behavioural factors would be an example of this type of program. Briggs and Mantini-Briggs (2003) in their account of a deadly outbreak of cholera in Venezuela aim to "provide everyone who is affected by social inequality, stigma, and disease – that is all of us – with new tools" to cope with vulnerabilities to illness. It is my hope to contribute to this project by looking at Dominican stories about HIV/AIDS.

This paper will take seriously the rumours about HIV/AIDS that were circulating during my first two prolonged periods of fieldwork in the Eastern Caribbean nation of Dominica (August 1996-August 1997 and October 1997-May 1998). The rumours were connected to the shift in Dominica's economic status from an agricultural producer to a service provider. This shift has been the direct result of neo-liberal economic policies and decisions made by the international economic community, specifically those that relate to the "banana wars." To take these rumours seriously, rather than dismissing these narratives as "false" or as evidence of "conspiracy theories," facilitates an examination of the socio-economic and historical context that gave rise to these widespread beliefs. In doing so, it is my hope that the counter-epistemic stories told by some of my interlocutors will help to contribute to our understanding of the connections between colonial exploitation, slavery, racism, current economic globalization, and the impact of an economic crisis on the health outcomes of the affected population. It is also my hope to help to contribute to the creation of more sensitive and efficacious health initiatives in the future.

Context

On June 23, 2000 an agreement between the European Community and its member states and members of the African, Caribbean and Pacific (ACP) group of states was signed in Cotonou, Benin. This agreement, known as the "Cotonou Agreement," will expire in 2020. The agreement temporarily extends the protection formerly afforded to ACP banana producers under Lomé IV.[1] However, most banana farmers in Dominica have little confidence in their economic future as is evidenced by the sharp and steady decline in banana production there. The Cotonou Agreement marked the final chapter in an ongoing trade dispute dubbed the "Banana Wars" by the news media. The "eight year standoff between the European Union and the USA over bananas" had dire consequences, especially for smaller Caribbean nations such as Dominica, St. Lucia, St. Vincent, and the Grenadines. (Myers 2004:1)

My fieldwork in Dominica from 1996 to 2001 focused on AIDS awareness education and prevention initiatives. From the time of my first arrival in Dominica in August of 1996, anxieties surrounding the then current trade dispute between the United States and the ACP nations over the protected banana trade, were a frequent topic of conversation and surfaced in discussions about HIV/AIDS (Rose 2005). The dispute stemmed from a complaint made to the WTO by the US Trade Representative over the long-standing agreement that allowed ACP nations special access to their former colonial metropole countries though a system of quotas and protected price agreements for banana export/import.

Around the world, people have "positioned the meaning of AIDS in relation to their structural positions in the local and global order" (Setel 1999:238) through various rumours and slogans that relate HIV/AIDS to asymmetrical and racist international relations. Paul Farmer (1992:230) has noted, "conspiracy theories have been a part of the AIDS scene since the advent of the syndrome." Allport and Postman (1945) define *rumour* as "a specific proposition for belief, passed along from person to person, usually by word of mouth, without secure standards of evidence being present." Rumours are unverified, orally transmitted narratives (Turner 1993:1). But rumours are more than incorrect or incomplete information. They are socially constructed, publicly performed, and publicly interpreted narratives. As such, rumours reflect and construct beliefs about how the world works at a particular place and time (Kroeger 2003; Fine 1992; Kapferer 1990). This article intends to treat "such local, disqualified forms of interpretation" (Palmié 2002:20) as "situated knowledge" – a

---

1   This is the name of the trade agreement that offered special, duty-free access for ACP (African, Caribbean and Pacific) bananas being imported into their former colonial metropole countries. In the case of Dominica and other islands that had been subject to British rule, this access was to the United Kingdom.

counter-epistemology that challenges ways of thinking and points to the increased marginalization brought on by neo-liberal economic policies. In doing so we can learn about the way the world looks to post-colonial subjects who continue to have little power in the current global arena.

A (Lost) Window of Opportunity

In 1996, UNAIDS had reported that the Caribbean was a "window of opportunity" – HIV/AIDS rates were relatively low and it was believed that intervention strategies would be effective in preventing a health crisis in the region. The AIDS epidemic was not yet at crisis level and there was optimism that effective AIDS prevention programs could be launched and a human crisis averted. At the same time, the United States Trade Representative had launched an official complaint against the preferential treatment afforded to African, Caribbean, and Pacific Bananas under the Lomé Protocol. Walking around Dominica I often heard snippets that alluded to the changes that the island nation was facing. At the hospital while waiting for my chest x-ray (a requirement for the visa) a woman commented, "Imagine, you have to pay to make a baby now!" She was referring to the newly introduced user fees at the hospital, a change made in response to IMF and World Bank demands. In Roseau, the capital, I saw a woman on a stool selling ripe bananas for 25 cents each. A man walked past her and commented loudly "What, we in the UK now? We have to PAY for banana?" As popular theatre workers and public health officials in Dominica toured the country providing AIDS prevention education, the populace was facing a massive economic crisis. The island was abuzz with talk about the two events – the arrival and increasing awareness of HIV ("de virus") and the impending collapse of their primary economic base. Indeed, during the Dominica fieldwork period from 1996-2001, there were two widely circulating popular narratives concerning HIV/AIDS. These narratives went against the public health and AIDS committee's efforts to provide AIDS education and prevention and reflected the people's growing concerns about the impending demise of their economy as a result of the US-led complaint against Dominica's protection of its principal export crop – bananas. The first narrative held that the United States, or the CIA, had manufactured the virus in a laboratory, with the intent of destroying the black (or poor) populations around the globe. Many Dominicans believed that condoms donated to the Dominican Planned Parenthood Association by USAID had been impregnated with HIV by "the Americans." This type of rumour was not unique to Dominica. Setel has reported that the people he worked with in Tanzania also circulated a story that American condoms were impregnated with HIV (Setel 1999:240). In Dominica, this rumour was made even more plausible by the belief that the supply of donated condoms had been decreased or halted entirely after the "discovery" that HIV/AIDS could be transmitted through heterosexual contact. According to this narrative, once the virus had been introduced into the population, the Americans had moved to the second phase of their attack by ensuring that the virus would spread. Here is an example of a conversation on this topic:

> Marna[2]: They used to send us condoms from the United States. The condoms went to town, to the family planning clinic on George Street. They told people to use them not to make babies – they said we were having too many babies.
>
> Barella: And it was true sometimes in those days it was babies having babies. And girls getting thrown out of school. So we thought it was a good thing.
>
> Marna: But then they got to know that the virus could be spread man to woman and woman to man. And then they stopped sending the condoms. It was then that they stopped sending the condoms. Remember in 1987 – was it? – that was the first time we heard about AIDS here.
>
> Barella: Yes, wi. It was then that we realized we had the virus here and it was the condoms that had the virus in them. That is how the virus came to Dominica.

We continued our conversation for while, with me expressing concern and some doubt that this would happen. It seemed too cruel, I said. Then Barella said, "But you see what they are doing now, Dee? Now they are taking our banana and it was only banana we had to get us anywhere in life." Marna choopsed loudly and then said, "They trying to kill us is all."

A second related belief was that information about HIV/AIDS disseminated by the news media and international development workers was a fabrication. The lie was concocted by "the Americans" (or an unnamed "them"), in order to trick black men into wearing condoms to thereby prevent the births of the next generation of Dominicans. People pointed out that USAID used to distribute condoms, through the Planned Parenthood Association, as a form of birth control. The distribution of free condoms, I was told, was halted once it became known that HIV could be spread through heterosexual contact. The variation of this narrative outlined above suggested that the imported condoms themselves had been "infected" or "dirty." These ideas fit a narrative wherein "Americans" wished to decrease the birth-rate of

---

2   Following standard anthropological practice, the names cited here are pseudonyms.

Dominicans – a future-oriented genocide. Again, this idea that AIDS does not exist is another common theme in AIDS rumours in the developing world. A commercial sex worker in the Dominican Republic town of Carrefour expressed the following beliefs when asked about HIV/AIDS:

> "AIDS!" Her lips curl about the syllable. "There is no such thing. It is a false disease invented by the American government to take advantage of poor countries. The American president hates poor people, so now he makes up AIDS to take away the little we have." [Selzer 1987:60]

Here is an example from Dominica. Although this conversation was a bit tongue and cheek, it provides a clear example of this type of narrative:

> Jacko: They do not want us anymore. They don't want us to have children. So they tell us there is this thing, the virus, and the condom will protect us from it. But you see, there is no virus. It is not true. We are made to think that we are protecting ourselves but really we are doing their work for them. They don't have to kill us. No more babies – no more Dominicans, you see? And you see they do that to their own too. Everywhere them want to do that.
>
> Me: Who?
>
> Jacko: You know them. Just look around. Just look at what they are doing to our bananas. Just look at them go on the boats to take the ganja. Just look, wi, just look.

The views he expressed to me that afternoon provide a very clear and concise narrative that links life, livelihood, and way of life. As in the conversation with Marna and Barbella, the narrative provides a poignant, and as I hope to now show, astute reading of global assymetries and realities crystalized for the people on this island with the banana wars. Put another way, while these rumours pose difficulties for AIDS education and prevention initiatives, particularly those that emphasize condom use as a form of protection, but, (as Treichler has pointed out):

> We can do other things with theories of AIDS than seek to eradicate them or, more pragmatically, circumvent them. As we look over the meanings that AIDS has generated as it moves among subcultures and around the globe, we can ask different kinds of questions. Who are cast as villains in a particular account of AIDS? How does a given account resonate with different constituencies? What's in it for its adherents? The widespread belief that AIDS is a deliberate experiment conducted on vulnerable populations is an example. In sub-Saharan Africa, the

idea is common that AIDS is the latest effort by white global elites to control the reproduction of people of color. [Treichler 1999:221]

The widespread notion that AIDS is an American invention "often reveals an unwelcome narrative about colonialism in a postcolonial world" (Treichler 1999:103). In Dominica, this narrative was tied to the processes of globalization underway there during the fieldwork period. My last example from fieldwork is not an example of AIDS denial but rather an example of one of the ways AIDS was understood as a syndrome tied to global inequality. The example is taken from a community theatre workshop held at the Roseau Waterfront Workers' Union Hall in November, 1997. The skit was a dramatization of the discussion that followed an AIDS prevention talk given by a public health nurse. It was one of several skits that evening, but one that is illustrative of a point. Since participation in these health workshops was voluntary it is reasonable to assume that the participants that evening were people who believed that HIV/AIDS did indeed exist. The dramatization was set between two households and a party. There were no props, but the scenes were indicated through dialogue and the movement of chairs in the space at the front of the hall. The characters were two mothers, portrayed by middle aged Dominican women, two daughters portrayed by younger women and a young man. The man, we were told, worked for a well-known cruise line:

> Two young women are talking about a party they plan to attend. One goes home and her mother asks her to sit down. "Lisa, come and sit with me a minute. I need to talk to you about something." The daughter sits and her mother tells her that she is hearing more and more about this virus, HIV. She tells her daughter that she must be very careful. If she goes with somebody, she must be very sure about him and should use protection. The daughter assures her mother that she will take care of herself and asks permission to go to a party with her friend. The mother says okay and tells her that she must be home by midnight. Then the action moves to the other side of the "stage," where Lisa's friend is telling her mother that she will be going to a party. The mother has no comment. The young women go to the party where they meet with a friend, a handsome young man who works on a cruise ship. After the party, both girls return to their respective homes. Lisa's mother is waiting up for her, angry that she is late, but happy to see her home and safe. The other mother is asleep or absent. The next day Lisa's mother sits her down for another talk. "Lisa I heard something and I'm afraid." She asks her daughter if she was at the party with the "handsome fellow from Fascination." "You know

Lisa, de boy is travelling north and south and east and west and they say he has de virus." She gives her daughter fifty dollars to "take de test and put my mind at ease." Lisa gets her friend, who was the one with the "fellow" and brings her to the clinic for an HIV test.

This performance highlights the sense of Dominica as an island and the connection between poverty, tourism, and HIV/AIDS (Lisa's friend agreed to go with the guy because she wanted Nikes for Carnival) in the transmission of HIV/AIDS emerges.

In order to understand how the rumours and assumptions described so far hold credence in Dominica, we need only look at the country's history and its current position in the global economy.

Colonial Legacies and Racism

Ignoring the past not only harms understanding of the present but compromises present action. [Bloch 1993:61]

For nearly 300 years, African bodies were purchased, kidnapped, transported, and sold as chattel. Slave traders stripped and displayed the Africans on blocks so that plantation owners or their agents could choose strong, healthy people to work as slaves on their plantations. On the plantations, slaves were forced to do strenuous labour and were subjected to corporal punishment, rape, and, occasionally, murder. The white elite displayed anxiety over African bodies, sexuality, and the "purity" of the white race – at least as far as relations between African men and European women were concerned (Beckles 1999; D'Emilio and Freedman 1997). Plantation owners also exhibited concern and control over the Africans' reproductive capacities. Thus, African bodies were subjected to scrutiny, legislation, and maltreatment in regard to both their productive and reproductive lives. Although none of the Dominicans that I spoke with referred to slavery when discussing HIV/AIDS as an American-invented tool for genocide, certainly all were aware of its legacy. For many Dominicans, satellite television, stories from friends and relatives overseas, and personal travel have reinforced the fact of racism.

People who believed that HIV/AIDS was a fabrication – a virus invented in an American laboratory to eliminate the black race or a lie concocted to trick black men into using condoms and preventing Dominican births – often pointed to contemporary racism in the United States. Dominica has high rates of emigration, and the most common destinations outside the Caribbean region are the United States,

Britain, and Canada. Many Dominicans have lived in one of these countries or have relatives who do. Posters of Reverend Doctor Martin Luther King, Jr., don the walls of many public places. With satellite television, many Dominicans saw the Rodney King beating. As one interlocutor commented, "You see what they do to their own. Imagine what they would do to us." However, by far, the most common association between HIV/AIDS and genocide was rooted in the looming crisis in the banana industry.

AIDS Rumours and the Political Economy

Dominica's agricultural economy is historically rooted in the slave-based plantation system of the French and British colonial regimes that controlled the country at one time or another. During the Plantation Era, the period of slavery, estates practiced monocrop agriculture for export to Europe and America. Slaves were given some basic provisions that included salt, salt cod or smoked herring, rudimentary clothing or fabric, and a ration of flour. They lived in chattel houses that they built themselves and were given a small plot of less desirable land on which they were required to grow the bulk of their own food, in addition to labouring in the fields. Any surplus remained the property of the slave who could then sell it at the marketplace on Sundays. Some people were able to purchase their freedom this way; others used the monies earned to purchase fabric to make dressy clothes or for foodstuffs or entertainment (Honychurch 1995; Rose 2009a; 2005). Today, people still refer to certain food items as "provisions."

Following the British Empire's emancipation of African slaves on August 1, 1834, newly freed slaves left the estates and established squatter settlements. Many freed men and women cultivated their own small plots, selling any surplus in the local markets. A marketing system was already in place as a result of the Sunday sales of surplus crops described above (cf Honychurch 1995). Archival sources highlight the reluctance of newly freed slaves to engage in contract labour for former slave owners. Indeed, much of Dominica's economic history in the period immediately after emancipation describes the numerous strategies employed by the colonial government and the planter class to try to force the new peasant class into wage labour for the estates. Michel-Rolph Trouillot (1988) has argued that the development of a peasantry in Dominica was a form of resistance that enabled people to maintain a level of independence by limiting their engagement with the cash economy. Former slaves continued to produce for subsistence, selling the surplus in the local market. The colonial government, mainly through the imposition of taxation, forced many individuals into wage labour on estates where they produced crops for export to the United Kingdom. Despite significant historical changes – for example, the shift from slavery to independent producers or wage labourers – the majority of the population remained in agricultural production, and Dominica has continued to export tropical fruits through both inter-island and international trade. Farmers also produce a surplus to sell to local hotels and in the Saturday markets in Roseau and Portsmouth. Early in the last century, bananas became the prominent export crop.

The economic crisis caused by the collapse of the banana industry was seen as a direct attack by the United States on the Caribbean. Indeed, many people did not even mention Chiquita, the multinational responsible for the complaint, but pointed directly to the United States. Television, newspapers, and conversations in public places spread the news that the US Trade Representative had lodged the complaint against the protocol protecting ACP bananas. For Dominicans, the banana industry represented more than potential economic security. It enabled many Dominicans to retain an independent lifestyle as peasant farmers. In short, it represented a form of freedom through the ability to retain a degree of independence from wage labour and the capacity to continue to grow subsistence crops while maintaining a reliable cash income. Secondly, despite the relative independence afforded to individual farmers, due to the country's reliance on a single crop (bananas) and, for the most part, a single market (the United Kingdom), the decline in the banana industry has been an economic disaster for the country (Rose 2009a:87-97). The economic crisis has meant increasing reliance on tourism and emigration; I will elaborate on these effects in the final section of this article. Throughout the AIDS prevention workshops that were the focus of my fieldwork, Dominicans repeatedly associated poverty, tourism, and emigration with HIV/AIDS.

The Crisis in Dominica's Banana Industry

Dominica is the poorest country in the English-speaking Caribbean and was so even before events in the world economy stifled their principal industry. Most Dominicans I encountered became angry when they heard reports of their country's poverty. Many of them told me, "We may not have money, but we have food." Twiggy, a young man who was about to attend college, asked me why Europeans, who have so much money, allow some to die of rickets and scurvy just for want of fruit. In Dominica, he assured me, such a thing could never happen. Despite its relative poverty, people in Dominica boast a high life expectancy and enjoy healthy diets, thanks to an abundance of fish, rainfall, and fertile land. In 1995, the new government responded to structural adjustment demands by introducing user fees at hospitals. Prior to that, most people had access to adequate health care services. Dominicans also share an ethos of caring. When a person (especially a child) requires health care that exceeds the capacity of Dominican facilities, community members collect money, and a few wealthy families contribute the balance to meet the costs of sending the patient overseas for treatment.

At the time of my fieldwork, 67 percent of the labour force was employed by the banana industry – primarily as peasant farmers, packers, truck drivers, or employees of the Dominican Banana Marketing Association. Many Dominicans engaged in multiple occupations. Some bus drivers doubled as tour guides when a cruise ship was in port, and many men also worked informally in this capacity. The tourist sector was a growing source of employment, hiring tour guides, taxi drivers, hotel workers, bartenders, servers, cleaners, receptionists, and souvenir vendors. The government and service sector were also major sources of employment. Women dominated in the marketplace and comprised the majority of the hucksters. They also sold sweets and snacks from street side stalls or from windows in their homes, took in laundry, and ran the majority of the island's rum shops and snackettes. There was also a small sector of professionals, including lawyers, doctors, engineers, and one psychologist. However, as noted earlier, the major economic sector was agriculture (Rose 2005).

Why Bananas?

Prior to 1930, the Dominican banana was not an export commodity. Bananas were consumed locally, and banana trees were used as shade trees for the principal export crops of cocoa and limes, which needed protection from the sun when immature. There was, however, a small scale inter-island trade in bananas shipped from Portsmouth, the major city and port on the northwest side of the island (Mourillon nd:9). However, in 1928 and 1930, Dominica was hit by hurricanes that destroyed the lime orchards, effectively putting an end to the lime industry because lime trees take up to eight years to resuscitate. In 1931, Mr. A.C. Shillingford found a market overseas and began to ship the Gros Michel banana to Liverpool on Leyland Line steamships.

The industry faced many challenges, however. For one thing, Dominica lacked sufficient roads, making it difficult for small holders in remote areas to get their produce to port. Another problem was that the Gros Michel variety of banana was susceptible to Panama disease. By 1937, the Canadian Banana Company was accepting only high-grade bananas free of scars. World War II brought problems in shipping, which stopped altogether in 1942 after the Canadian National Steamship boats were destroyed by enemy action. The British government stepped in with a wartime subsidy to "relieve small-holders, who had been depending exclusively on bananas for a livelihood" (Mourillon nd:13). These trends – the demand for high-quality, unblemished bananas and the granting of subsidies to ensure Dominican smallholders continued to produce bananas – remained in place until the World Trade Organization (WTO) ruling in 2000.

One of the factors that led to the adoption of the banana crop as a staple export was that there was an existing market in Europe and North America. From a geopo-litical and economic standpoint, a number of factors combined to create this market. Beginning in the nineteenth century, the new mass transportation technologies of steamship and rail, along with the availability of cheap land and labour in the tropics combined to make the banana a viable economic investment. The processes of indus-trialization, the development of mass markets in Europe and North America, and the rise of multinational corporations led to the exploitation and consumption of this new commodity (Nurse and Sandiford 1995:1). Another factor was the weakening sugar industry (Nurse and Sandiford 1995:26). The presence of an existing market and the decline of another major export crop were significant factors in Dominica's turning to bananas for export – but there were other reasons as well.

From an ecological standpoint, the banana is a viable plant because it is peren-nial, it grows well on steep slopes, its canopy provides shade for other plants that are grown between the rows of banana trees, the refuse from the tree provides mulch, and it has a relatively high yield per acre (Nurse and Sandiford 1995:16). Another important benefit of the banana tree is that it has a short nine-month gestation period, so growers can quickly rehabilitate it after hurricane damage (Nurse and Sandiford 1995:78). Thus, the crop is well suited to Dominica's ecological niche. Finally, since the majority of Dominica's banana producers are smallholders, they produce for their own subsistence, as well as for the market. "Fig" or green bananas have been and continue to be a staple in most Dominican's diets and are served in some households as a side dish with all meals. Nurse and Sandiford point to the peasant farmers' subsistence ethic of "safety first" and "risk aversion." As we have seen, an established market for bananas was already in place. As a perennial, the banana crop gave farmers a regular biweekly income (Nurse and Sandiford 1995:79).

Dominica's agricultural sector has been dominated by smallholders with 78 percent of the farms being less than 5 acres and fewer than 1 percent over 100 acres in size (Thomas 1996:247). Although the "Cotonou Agreement" (2002) promised a temporary reprieve for banana producers, most farmers in Dominica have little confidence in its effectiveness, as evidenced by the sharp and steady decline in banana production there. As Campbell notes:

> Although agriculture remains the leading contributor to Gross Domestic Product (GDP), the relative strength of its contribution in the 1990's is much lower than in the 1980's (IICA, 1997). ... Between 1988–1999 the banana industry of Dominica recorded a 63 percent decline in production and a 62 percent decline in export value. There was also a corresponding decline in the number of farmers and acreage under bananas. Many farmers have abandoned their fields, especially those dependent on labor. Rural employment has fallen and there is evidence of declining livelihood among rural households as a result of falling financial resources that engenders a reduction to access of goods and services they previously enjoyed. At the national level, Dominica has now moved from a position of net exporter of agri-food products to net importer ... and it is very likely that this situation will continue because of the openness of the economy and the changing food habits of the population. [Campbell 2001]

The decline in banana production marks a significant change for Dominicans. For most of its recorded history, Dominica has been the provider of agricultural crops for metropole countries. Dominican farmers have also grown the bulk of their own subsistence crops. Since emancipation, much of this farming has taken place on independent peasant farms, and a culture has emerged that is based upon relative independence from the cash economy, self-sufficiency, and an ethos of respect and caring (Rose 2005; 2009a:71-79). The crisis in the banana industry, therefore, marks more than an economic disaster. In the economic realm, there have been five interrelated results. There has been an increase in poverty levels; farmers and their families have been forced to emigrate in search of economic opportunities; land is increasingly alienated from the agricultural sector; and there is an increase reliance on imported goods. Anthropological and epidemiological evidence shows a correlation between these outcomes and the growing tourism trade. These studies also indicate that "poverty seems to favour rapid sexual spread of HIV" (Farmer 1995:3). Finally there is ample evidence linking tourism and HIV/AIDS (eg Farmer 1992; Padilla 2007). Thus, AIDS rumours in Dominica are "undisciplined stories" that deserve our attention.

HIV/AIDS and the Political Economy in Dominica: The Current Situation

According to a recent IMF report, rates of poverty in Dominica have increased significantly with 29 percent of households and 40 percent of the general population living in poverty, an increase of nearly 2 percent between 1995 and 2002 (IMF 2004). Alarmingly, 11 percent of households and 15 percent of the general population live in indigent poverty, and an average of 50 percent of Dominica's children live in poverty. In rural areas, one in every two households is poor. More than 37 percent of households in Dominica do not have access to piped water, and 25 percent of households have no access to toilet facilities. The situation is expected to worsen as the population faces increasing unemployment, which increased from 15.7 percent in 1999 to 25 percent in 2002. Along with poverty, the report mentions a rise in the number of cases of persons affected with tuberculosis – an indication of a corresponding increase in HIV/AIDS infections. Another development report on the socio-economic conditions in Dominica states, "Teenage pregnancy and reproductive health patterns of unprotected sex and gender-related issues have also been cited as problematic for Dominica. Dominica's current health situation sends a clear signal that HIV/AIDS prevention and education is becoming increasingly vital" (UNDP 2007).

The report concludes that Dominica is facing an economic crisis and that the country's "medium-term economic future rests on fiscal stability, tourism, and growth within the agricultural sector (specifically banana output)." The report links "social outcomes" to the fate of the banana industry, but pessimistically adds,

> Decreasing preferential access to the EU market for bananas and hurricane-related crop damage has made it difficult for Dominica to assert its position on the future of an uncertain banana industry. Dominica's banana exports fell by 38.5% to a record low of 10,563 tons in 2003. Dominica's attempt to diversify the agricultural market by a scarcity of agricultural labor, investment capital, and transportation costs.

The scarcity of agricultural labour is tied to the numbers of banana farmers who have left the country in search of economic opportunities elsewhere. Finally,

> In the near to medium term, tourism is expected to be the principal driver in the economy. While Dominica's tourism earnings averaged 18% of GDP compared to an average 29% in other islands, tourism contributes over 30% of Dominica's

foreign exchange earnings, three times the current earnings from bananas. In order to expand its tourism industry, Dominica will need to develop a coherent marketing strategy to promote its niche market – rainforests, waterfalls, volcanic sites and coral reefs – to the growing international eco-tourism market.

Rumours or Predictions?

In 1996, UNAIDS referred to the Caribbean as a "window of opportunity" referring to the perceived ability of development and health workers to prevent the spread of HIV and AIDS in the region, averting a pandemic such as that found in sub-Saharan Africa. Today the Caribbean has the second highest number of HIV/AIDS cases per capita in the world, and is ranked as the most affected sub-region in the Americas (Bryan 2007:60).

The intent of this article has been to focus attention on AIDS rumours as commentaries about the political and economic situation in Dominica, rather than to examine the profile of HIV/AIDS in the country. AIDS workers, local commentators, and development agencies all recognize the population's likely vulnerability to the virus. The concern is supported by ethnographic evidence and epidemiological analyses of HIV/AIDS in the region which, at least since Paul Farmer's (1992) groundbreaking work on the AIDS pandemic in Haiti, clearly demonstrate the link between poverty, tourism, and HIV/AIDS in the region (Farmer 1992, 1995; Forsythe 1999; Figueroa and Brathwaite 1995; Padilla 2007). In November 2006, Dominica's HIV/AIDS Unit launched its "Know Your Status" campaign to encourage voluntary HIV testing in the country (Laurent 2006). A report issued by the European Commission in December 2008 states that "Dominica is reported to have the second highest seroprevalence rate in the English-speaking Caribbean" (European Commission 2008). Even more alarming, reported figures do not necessarily reflect the HIV status of those many Dominicans who have migrated to more popular tourist destinations in search of work. Of 306 HIV positive persons living in Dominica in 2006, only 24 were getting ARV treatment and only 32 were accessing any form of health care (OECS 2006:6). Further, AIDS prevention and health outreach programs have been cut (European Commission 2008). The actual level of the problem is uncertain. What is certain is that the crisis in the banana industry has thrown an already impoverished nation into a widespread economic crisis with dire social, cultural, and health outcomes.

Structural violence renders populations vulnerable to certain types of illness and members of these communities are well aware of their historical, economic and political marginality. In the 1990s this awareness manifested in AIDS rumours circulating in vulnerable populations around the world, particularly in the Caribbean, sub-Saharan Africa, and the Southern United States. Today it is surfacing in narratives about the H1N1 flu strain. Rumours of vaccinations causing sterility are also widespread (Kaler 2009) and linked to conditions similar to those described above for Dominica. With news of a potentially efficacious HIV vaccine on the horizon, the implications of this material for health initiatives need be taken seriously. Programs that use "cultural strategies" are also of questionable value. Although it was not the focus of this paper, AIDS initiatives (foreign run) that pointed to Dominican cultural attributes (the common practice of men having multiple girlfriends, the difficulty some Dominican women reported in consistent condom use on the part of their partners) were simply dismissed out of hand: "We've always been this way, AIDS just came now." The discourse of public health workers, AIDS prevention and awareness activists, and Dominican media usually pointed to a link with a foreigner – HIV positive persons were reported and talked about only when they were people who had returned from another country with the virus, the first recorded case was always described as referring to the test results of a "foreigner who brought the virus to the island." Rather than understanding these narratives as a form of resistance or in any other way determined by the voice of outsiders, I am trying to make a case for taking these as commentaries or a kind of counter-epistemology about past relationships – colonialism, slavery, racism and the like, and their continuation in the form of neoliberal economic policies that are, once again, catered to the needs of those in power, those who are structurally associated with the global north.

To sum up, shifting position in the global economy – from agricultural producers to pleasure providers – constitutes both dramatic change and continuity. The conditions of survival are still predicated upon the demands and desires of the developed North. Finally, the link between AIDS and tourism in the region has been well-established (Farmer 1992; Padilla 2007). Yet development initiatives consistently insist upon tourism as part of the region's solution to widespread economic crises. AIDS prevention education is indeed called for in this context, yet education initiatives that emphasize cultural practices and promote condom use will only be of limited effectiveness as the AIDS narratives discussed above indicate. Rather than dismissing these stories as mere "rumour," we should perhaps pay closer attention to the critiques of global geopolitics and economics embedded within these narratives. What is really called for in terms of global change is likely beyond the province of mainstream development agencies, yet I am certain that the farmers and former farmers in Dominica would have some useful suggestions.

Acknowledgements

I would like to thank Gregory Cameron and Renee Sylvain for comments on earlier drafts of this paper and the anonymous reviewers for their helpful suggestions; Michael Lambek and Richard Lee for their guidance in the early days of fieldwork; and most of all, I would like to extend my heartfelt gratitude to the people of Dominica. *Tchembe wed!*

References

Allport, Gordon W. and Leo J. Postman
    1945   The Basic Psychology of Rumor. Transactions of the New York Academy of Sciences, Series II 8: 61- 81. Reprinted in Readings in Social Psychology (3rd edn.). Eleanor E. Maccoby, Theodore M. Newcomb & Eugene L. Hartley, eds. 1959. London: Methuen.

Beckles, Hilary McD.
    1999   Centering Woman: Gender Discourses in Caribbean Slave Society. Kingston: Ian Randle Publishers.

Bloch, Marc
    1993   Apologie pour l'histoire ou Métier d'historian. Paris: Armand Colin. (1st ed 1949).

Briggs, Charles with Clara Mantini-Briggs
    2003   Stories in the Time of Cholera: Racial Profiling During a Medical Nightmare. Berkeley: University of California Press.

Brummelhuis, Han ten and Gilbert Herdt (eds.)
    1995   Culture and Sexual Risk: Anthropological Perspectives on AIDS. New York: Routledge.

Bryan, Anthony T.
    2007   Sustainable Caribbean Tourism: Challenges and Growth to 2020. *In* No Island is an Island: The Impact of Globalization on the Commonwealth Caribbean. Gordon Baker, ed. Pp 44-78. London: Chatham House.

Campbell, Dunstan
    2001   Positioning Dominica's Agriculture for Sustained Economic and Social Development. Electronic document, http://www.uwichill.edu.bb/bnccde/dominica/conference/papers/CampbellD.html, accessed March 7 2003.

D'Emilio, John and Estelle B. Freedman
    1997   Intimate Matters: A History of Sexuality in America. 2nd edition. Chicago: University of Chicago Press.

European Commission
    2008   Development and Relations with African, Caribbean, and Pacific States. Country Strategy Papers, Dominica. Electronic document, http://ec.europa. eu/development/icenter/repository/scanned_dm_csp10_en.pdf, accessed January 24, 2009.

Farmer, Paul
    1992   AIDS and Accusation: Haiti and the Geography of Blame. Berkeley and Los Angeles: University of California Press.
    1995   Culture, Poverty, and the Dynamics of HIV Transmission in Rural Haiti. *In* Culture and Sexual Risk: Anthropological Perspectives on AIDS. Han ten Brummelhuis and Gilbert Herdt, eds. Pp 3-28. New York: Routledge.

Fine, G. A.
    1992   Manufacturing Tales: Sex and Money in American Culture. Knoxville: University of Tennessee Press.

Figueroa, J. P. and A. R. Brathwaite
    1995   Is Under-reporting of AIDS a Problem in Jamaica? The West Indian Medical Journal 44(2):51-4.

Forsythe, S.
    1999   HIV AIDS and Tourism. AIDS Analysis Africa.

Honychurch, Lennox
    1995   The Dominica Story. London: MacMillan Education Limited.

Inter-American Institute for Cooperation in Agriculture (IICA)
    1997   Agriculture in Dominica – Sector Profile.

International Monetary Fund (IMF)
    2004   Dominica: Interim Poverty Reduction Strategy Paper. IMF Country Report Number 04/7. Electronic document, http://www.imf.org/external/pubs/ft/ scr/2004/cr0407.pdf, accessed October 18 2008.

Kaler, Amy
    2009   Health Interventions and the Persistence of Rumour: The Circulation of Sterility Stories in African Public Health Campaigns. Social Science & Medicine 68(9):1711-9.

Kapferer, Jean-Noel
    1990   Rumors: Usage, Interpretations, and Images. New Brunswick NJ: Transaction Publishers.

Kroeger, Karen A.
    2003   AIDS Rumors, Imaginary Enemies, and the Body Politic in Indonesia. American Ethnologist 30(2):243-257.

Laurent, Malaika

    2006   'Know Your Status' HIV/AIDS campaign launches in Dominica. Caribbean Net News. Electronic document, http://www.caribbeannewsnow.com/carib-net/cgi-script/csArticles/articles/000044/004401.htm, accessed March 12 2010.

Mourillon, V.J. Francis

    nd   The Dominica Banana Industry from Inception to Independence 1928 -1978. Printed by Tropical Printers Ltd. W.I.

Myers, Gordon

    2004   Banana Wars, the Price of Free Trade. London: Zed Books.

Nurse, Keith & Wayne Sandiford

    1995   Windward Islands Bananas – Challenges and Options under the Single European Market. Jamaica: Friedrich Ebert Stiftung.

Organization of Eastern Caribbean States (OECS)

    2006   Scaling Up Prevention Care And Treatment to Combat the HIV/AIDS Pandemic in the Organization of Eastern Caribbean States. Annual Report for the Period of March 1st 2005-August 31 2006. Electronic document, http://www.oecs.org/Documents/GFATM%20annual%20report.pdf, accessed January 24, 2009.

Padilla, Mark

    2007   Caribbean Pleasure Industry: Tourism, Sexuality and AIDS in the Dominican Republic. Chicago: University of Chicago Press.

Palmié, Stephan

    2002   Wizards and Scientists: Explorations in Afro-Cuban Modernity and Tradition. Durham: Duke University Press.

Rose, Deidre

    2005   Morality Plays: Popular Theatre for AIDS Awareness in the Commonwealth of Dominica, WI. Doctoral Dissertation, University of Toronto.

    2009a   Bouyon Kultur: Creolization and Culture in Dominica. Dubuque: Kendall/Hunt

    2009b   Telling Treasure Tales: Commemoration and Consciousness in Dominica. Journal of American Folklore 122(484):127-147.

Selzer, Richard

    1987   A Mask on the Face of Death. Life 10(8):58-64.

Setel, Philip W.
    1999   A Plague of Paradoxes: AIDS, Culture and Demography in Northern
            Tanzania. Chicago: The University of Chicago Press.
Thomas, Clive
    1996   Three Decades of Agriculture in the Commonwealth Caribbean. *In* The
            Critical Tradition of Caribbean Political Economy: The Legacy of George
            Beckford. Kari and Michael Witter, eds. Jamaica: Ian Randle Publishers.
Treichler, Paula A.
    1999   How to Have Theory in an Epidemic: Cultural Chronicles of AIDS. Durham:
            Duke University Press.
Trouillot, Michel-Rolph
    1988   Peasants and Capital: Dominica in the World Economy. Baltimore: The John
            Hopkins University Press.
Turner, Patricia A
    1993   I Heard it Through the Grapevine: Rumor in African American Culture.
            Berkeley: University of California Press.
UNAIDS
    1997; 2006 Report on the Global HIV/AIDS Epidemic. Geneva: World Health
            Organization. United Nations Development Report (UNDP), Barbados
            Country Profile: Dominica. Electronic document, http://www.bb.undp.
            org/index.php?page=dominica, accessed October 15 2008.

Part Three

Putting Words into Action

A Reflection on Political Research and Social Justice Organizing

Anna L. Anderson-Lazo

The central fact for me is, I think, that the intellectual is an individual endowed with a faculty for representing, embodying, articulating a message, a view, an attitude, philosophy or opinion to, as well as for, a public. And this role has an edge to it, and cannot be played without a sense of being someone whose place it is publicly to raise embarrassing questions, to confront orthodoxy and dogma (rather than to produce them, to be someone who cannot easily be co-opted by governments and corporations, and whose raison d'etre is to represent all those people and issues that are routinely forgotten or swept under the rug. The intellectual does so on the basis of universal principles: that all human beings are entitled to expect decent standards of behaviour concerning freedom and justice from worldly power or nations, and that deliberate or inadvertent violations of these standards need to be testified and fought against courageously. Edward Said 1996:11-12

Introduction

This article began as my contribution to a conversation about political activism and engaged anthropology among colleagues who were increasingly uneasy with the actions of an aggressively pro-war administration in the U.S., and how the recent, future and ongoing effects of these neoimperialist aggressions would impact the contexts where anthropologists teach and conduct socially committed research, here and abroad. As I reflected on this fraught intersection and our tense historical moment,

I began to consider whether my recent work as a social justice organizer in the U.S. had shifted my understanding of the roles, responsibilities and relationships that characterize politically-engaged, ethnographic inquiry. Initially, I hoped that a thick description of the grassroots organizing models used by labour, faith-based and social justice organizations in the U.S. would shed light on recent discussions that seek to move the discipline toward a decolonizing anthropological praxis; however, I found that my own trajectory, shifting from engaged researcher to employed activist, reintroduced many of the epistemological, methodological and ethics-related questions and frustrations that I had interrogated so vigorously during my graduate training, fieldwork and ethnographic writing since the mid-1990s.

In what follows, I reflect on how the challenges I experienced as a conscientiously, engaged anthropologist in Guatemala articulate with those I encountered as a social justice organizer in San Diego, specifically employing the methods/processes for mobilizing collective action as I was trained by the PICO Institute. While some readers might contend or fear that this comparative approach aimed at producing constructive dialogue among activists and anthropologists who promote progressive social change dangerously decontextualizes the PICO model, I endeavour to situate carefully two sites of power/knowledge production in relation to both activist trajectories as well as to key counterhegemonic, disciplinary attempts to reconstruct methodologies and analysis as tools for social change. By making practice, power, research, and action the subjects of my analysis, I employ a postcolonial feminist critique, which interrogates the social location of the researcher, resists binary logics of praxis/theory, and locates the structural-material effects of ethnographic research within a broader field of power.

Insider and Outsider Dilemmas of an Apprentice Activist-Researcher

As a doctoral researcher in Guatemala in the late 1990s, my fieldwork among Garifuna – that is, Afro-indigenous, Black Carib – community leaders, activists and historians who were contributing to the democracy-building projects of the Guatemalan National Peace Process anticipated and raised some of the familiar qualms about the methods and ethics of conducting research in developing nations and among structurally peripheralized groups, especially in the context of political terror and violence, which seemed at the time of the so-called "Peace" to be escalating rather than subsiding. Initially, my research objective was to advance the understanding of how Garifuna people used their long-term, regional and transcommunal social networks and new legal right to a Garifuna-specific indigenous worldview, or *cosmovisión*, to refract their needs and concerns through the lenses crafted and imposed by distant architects – i.e., the United Nations proctoring the Peace Process and the putatively democratic governance apparatus, an alliance of the new government, the guerrilla, the military, and representatives of the three major Indigenous groups. This approach used participant observation and direct engagement with community scholars to critically reassess the usefulness of previous (often colonizing and empiricist) social scientific studies perennially focused on the "disappearance" and shallow (neoteric) roots of Garifuna culture, the persistence of the matrifocal family and religious traditions, the emphasis of Garifuna heritage on their indigenous linguistic background rather than their preponderantly African ancestry (which had been examined incessantly for more than fifty years), and, particularly salient during the Peace Process, the alleged lack of political participation among Garifuna communities in their home countries throughout Central America since the 19th century.

At the outset, however, my Garifuna interlocutors raised their own, community-specific concerns about outsider anthropologists, especially those from the U.S., conducting field research that contributed little to and often impeded their everyday lives and ongoing political struggles, and they proscribed research activities for me that would meet their needs. In a related vein, they also expressed a growing fear that, beyond a handful of over-utilized professionals, they were inadequately prepared to take advantage of new democratic and development opportunities. For nearly two years, then, at the invitation of Garifuna political leaders, activists and organizers, I attended almost daily Peace Process meetings officiated by government officials, NGO workers and representatives of the UN or participated in other social, cultural and political gatherings organized by community groups, with my notes serving to inform those who were not able to attend. Various Garifuna community leaders also suggested that I should visit several learned elders, which I did weekly, to record a Garifuna community history that proclaimed their worldview as the basis for their survival of a civil war that spanned a period of four decades as well as for their resistance to the systematic, structural and racial marginalization of their community over two centuries. These combined activities gave me a sense that my research was respectfully conceived and community-driven, but I frequently encountered the need to clarify my role and my aims. Specifically, I emphasized that I was a student apprenticing in both research and political work, attempting to make my modest institutional and intellectual resources available to the community.

As I describe and situate more extensively in the dissertation (2003), I began to inhabit the role of an apprentice – that is, working in the company of experts and elders to learn about and identify community need; using anthropology to support community efforts; and planning to be transformed by this experience of living among people who were actively seeking to change the historical, cultural and structural conditions that had caused a protracted genocidal civil war and produced a deeply stratified society riddled with poverty, illiteracy, and disease to which they were exceedingly vulnerable. Thus, as my relationships with community members deepened, I sought an anthropological role that placed in the foreground my own trajectory as a young woman of working class, mixed cultural background, African-descended and Native American, whose research interests in community organizing and political practice echoed but, more importantly, could build on my commitments and capacities as an anti-colonial, feminist and social justice activist-researcher. I found that I was seeking more than merely rapport; rather I was working toward research as an intellectual collaboration based on political solidarity with Garifuna community organizers.

Among the various conditions that made my social location relevant and complex, I observed that being a relatively young, female researcher, who was often misrecognized by outsiders as a Garifuna participant or representative, offered both advantages and obstacles for me and the people with whom I was conducting my research, especially as community leaders began to use strategically my credentials, expertise and institutional relationships to advance the aims of their organizations and projects. Some fieldwork situations seemed straightforward, even easy, such as using my tutorial in Garifuna language to assist in the funding and development of the first draft of a national bilingual curriculum; however other situations were more nuanced. For instance, midway through my research when I received a Fulbright grant to support my research, I was truly grateful for the funding and other substantial forms of support offered by the program; however I also felt compelled to express my ambivalence about participating in a program that was conceived, largely, to project the "nice face of US imperialism" in the world. Garifuna leaders, however, welcomed and used my connections to the embassy, especially the cultural program assistance provided by the US Information Agency, to amplify their presence through more, positive representations of themselves in the capital. Similarly in another instance, Garifuna leaders strongly encouraged me to participate alongside government ministers and entrepreneurs from several countries in a meeting to advance the development of the Bay of Honduras region as a site of cultural tourism from which Garifuna representatives were expressly excluded, and when my turn to speak arrived, I was told that time had run out so I should simply introduce myself. Noting that I was the youngest, only non-white and female person in the room, I took the opportunity to leverage my citizenship and status as a US Fulbright scholar, stating that my research addressed the crucial significance of the Garifuna to the settling and economic development of the Caribbean lowlands since colonial times, which in that instant became the subject of a chapter in the dissertation I was soon to write.

Again, readers might apprehend the reflexive stance I employ in this essay as a naive reintroduction of advocacy anthropology or as C.R. Menzies describes the latter, anthropology "on behalf," as a remedy to colonial/colonizing research paradigms that long produced knowledge about oppressed peoples for the sake of the powerful (2001). Rather I agree with Menzies, that research is always, already political, and as I discuss at length in the section comparing social justice organizing and engaged ethnographic inquiry, I concur with him, that the final stage consisting of writing, analysis, revision and distribution is the most important for ensuring that the product of one's research is respectfully engaged (2001:22). My attempts to engage my interlocutors in the design and execution of my research plan were manifold; nonetheless, I found that politically engaged work requires a concerted transgression of hegemonic research norms that extend well beyond the field project. For instance, when I was preparing to leave Livingston, Guatemala in late 1998, I organized a community conference where I would present my initial research findings and receive comments from the community at large as well as a panel of leaders, elders and scholars. I received feedback that intimated the high hopes that my friends, allies and acquaintances had for me. Specifically, they stated that I should more than merely publish their stories, which they thought would benefit me and to a lesser degree help to advance some of their more politically-expedient critiques of anthropological research, but rather they hoped that I would mature as a scholar-activist and perhaps continue to work for their community by forming a development NGO that strengthened their ties to the United States and other transnational entities. While I had a well-rehearsed, postcolonial analysis of development (cf. Escobar 1995) as well as a feminist critique of the NGOization of Latin American social movements (cf. Alvarez 1998), I understood this as a call to action on a deep level that would require more than composing a document that acknowledged the concerns expressed by my Garifuna interlocutors.

My readings, conversations and work alongside other anti-colonial activists and academics in Guatemala and in the US encouraged me to carefully choose subjects that reproduce neither hegemonic categories of difference nor the hierarchies of domination they obscure. More specifically, my feminist training charged me to see my subjective, embodied experience as part of my research (cf., Zavella 1997); and considering the multiplicity of selves (Abu-Lughod 1990; 1991) that arises in the shifting contexts where I conduct action-research, I take up the challenge of post-structural anthropology to understand the texts I produce as constitutive of real, material effects, including producing knowledge to be shared across activist trajectories and interest groups. When, for instance, I shifted my focus, as Alexander and Mohanty (1997) suggest, from reproducing a category such as "people in struggle" or "women organizers" to advancing a transhistorical understanding of the "work" of organizing that recognizes how common social change goals and activist trajectories can create linkages with other social change "workers," I began to propose that my research might produce transgressive, (perhaps) decolonizing analysis to undermine the intractable insider/outsider dynamics that have required the perennial reinvention, recapturing and retrofitting of anthropology, cultural critique and social analysis (Hymes 1969; Marcus and Fisher 1986; Rosaldo 1989). My hope, as an anthropologist trained in the 1990s, is that new interventions can make use of these key reflexive moments in the discipline to genuinely shift paradigms of praxis in relation to new conceptual frameworks, such as intersectionality, transcommunality, and transnational feminisms, and shared domains of knowledge production and activism.

The Personal is Political: Activist Trajectories and Professional Organizing

During the early 2000s when U.S. progressives were considering how to respond to the fact that despite our protests the far-right effectively had taken control of the federal administration, legislative and executive branches alike, to launch a world-wide, ideological and material war in the name of democracy and freedom both in our "homeland" and everywhere beyond, I finished the long process of writing the dissertation. Frankly, I felt personally accomplished, yet politically disconnected from the United States and the people in Guatemala, whose interests I had hoped to support with my newly minted PhD. To my professional chagrin, I also realized that I was experiencing what many previous anthropologists have lived: the literal and relational distancing of the researcher from the subjects with whom they conduct research. I began to consider seriously again the suggestion made by Garifuna elders that marginalized communities needed more professionals who are prepared to run organizations, participate in civil society, and government, and I examined how the relatively privileged educational experience that had (literally) saved me from my impoverished roots, had done little to prepare me to be a powerful political actor on my own behalf, much less in solidarity with the people in Guatemala from whom I had received so much.

Thus I found appealing the opportunity to work directly with communities on the U.S.-Mexico border, where I thought my citizenship conferred decidedly "insider" rights and responsibilities that would facilitate my understanding of political power and contextualize my role as an anthropologist within a broader consciousness of historical trajectories of activisms in the United States. Consequently, in San Diego, I took a job as the development director (writing grants and fundraising) for a non-profit organization that focused on using Internet and other technologies to support progressive community building, networking and activism across the 11 villages that make up a sprawling, metropolitan, and largely stratified and segregated city. In this work with its focus on progressive interconnectivity, I found that a host of organizations sought to represent low-income Latino immigrant and African-American peoples in the region, but few actually engaged them in the process. Within a year of moving to San Diego, I was offered a job as a bilingual community organizer with the San Diego Organizing Project (SDOP), a faith-based community organization serving 45,000 families in the region, which had established a strong track record of recruiting and training community leaders and building alliances with progressive organizations, elected officials and working-class constituencies. As a member of what previously had been called the Pacific Institute for Community Organizing (now more succinctly the PICO National Network), representing one million families in 150 cities and 17 states, SDOP worked on social justice issues at the local, regional and national level as part of "one of the largest community-based efforts in the United States." After 35 evaluative interviews with the community leaders for whom I would work as an organizer, I was hired to mobilize five congregations to address social justice issues, including housing, employment, development, immigration rights, education, neighborhood safety, healthcare and environmental quality.

Many contemporary faith-based social justice organizations claim, as SDOP/PICO does in its training manual, that "churches are among the few organizations that can span the whole range of public and private relationship," and that "faith-based organizing is a means of reestablishing a public voice for people" (PICO Manual N.d.). Admittedly, as I considered what organizing work among religious groups would entail, it was easy for me to cast churches based in the US as hegemonic ideological institutions steeped in a colonial legacy, while the Afro-Catholic mutual aid societies with whom I had worked in Guatemala were easier to situate as libratory groups that had successfully transgressed the repression and genocidal pograms of the counterinsurgency during the civil war. Furthermore, when a prominent San Diego organizer explained that the organizational motto, "never do for people, what they can do for themselves," implies "teaching people to do community development," I contemplated how applicable postcolonial critiques of development frameworks would be for me as an organizer. Therefore, as I fought to resist a cozy armchair approach that would pit well-positioned theory against action on the ground, I was forced to confront the fact that my kneejerk fears arose from my relative ignorance of US faith-based organizing history. Thus, my employment offered an opportunity for me to investigate the "work" of organizing in a new social, historical context, to interrogate my own "will to activism" in relation to social change trajectories "at home," and to examine how organizing models much like rather than in conflict with anthropological frameworks, address similar concerns about research, engagement, analysis, action and power.

In an interview in 2007, a PICO national director explained that the PICO model applies "social network theory," which means that they focus on developing community leaders to raise concerns that can be addressed through the political process in "multiple arenas." He described how they are currently testing their capacity at the national level, by posing the following question: "can a non-hierarchal, grassroots, network movement impact national policy?" While this question seemed mostly rhetorical at the time, I would venture an affirmative answer. Contemporary social movements in the U.S. draw on a deep, historical legacy of successful grassroots political mobilization from previous movements here and abroad, and, clearly, the PICO organizing model builds on a particularly rich intersection of activist trajectories.

Thus, by citing such influences as Liberation Theology in Latin America and the work of such figures as Paolo Freire, Deborah Meier (1995), as well as Anne Hope and Sally Timmel, U.S. organizations invoke a body of transnational organizing thought that acknowledges the interconnection and multidirectional flows among these movements and trajectories. As an organizer for two years, which involved direct relationship-building with the community leaders from the five churches I was employed to support as well as four years of conducting formal and informal ethnographic interviews among participants engaged in activism across a range of non-profit groups, unions and NGOs focused on organizing or civic voluntarism, I found that the most prominent, local and national groups historicizing a specific framework or "model" for mobilizing collective action among faith-based communities explicitly cited the influence of civil rights church groups, trade unionism and the lifework of Saul Alinsky (especially 1971). This trajectory, of course, draws the connection of church-based movements to explicitly class-based struggle. Alinsky's criminology research in the late 1930s among youth in the "Back-of-the-Yards" area of Chicago led him, first, to transgress his received role as a silent observer, and secondly to develop a model for creating what he called "an organization of organizations" that would engage working class communities in the political process (see Skocpol 2000; Whitman 2006). The entity he created eventually became the IAF, a strong, secular national network that today mobilizes grassroots collective action in similar ways to PICO in the United States. While various political analysts suggest that in the context of a decline of (participation in) the public sphere, especially since the 1980s, these organizations, like other neopopulist schemes, have "run up against the limits of their own localist parochialism and inertia" (Boggs 1997:759), others seek to ground historically an argument that these efforts continue to build powerful social change forces by equipping an engaged citizenry to make use of new solidarities and activism at state and national levels of governance (Wood 2007).

In this vein, a brief though not shallow, recent history of organizing in the United States recognizes the Civil Rights Movement in large part as a church-based movement, producing new political phenomena, such as the Southern Christian Leadership Conference (SCLC), which served as an umbrella organization of affiliates from various sectors. An array of social science studies explores the intersections of religion with other arenas of public life that point back to the political realm. For instance, examinations of the role of women in changing and politicizing the Black Church (Higgenbotham 1993; 1996) should be linked to the role of these same women in forging national feminist alliances and founding powerful organizations such as NOW, which continues to be construed as a solely white/second wave feminist group (Braude 2004). Other studies show how contemporaneous developments such as Vatican II and the Civil Rights Movement brought about changes in the U.S. that made the Catholic Church a site of social change mobilization, resonating with grassroots social action such as Liberation Theology throughout Latin America. Thus, one might broaden the historical lens for church-based organizing to reexamine such occurrences as the election of the first Catholic U.S. president in relation to the passing of the Civil Rights Act of 1964; to Robert Kennedy's support of the UFW in 1966; and to the emergence of Dr. King's "Poor People's Campaign," but more importantly, we might use these intersections of political and religious life to identify emerging transcommunal, social protest/social change frameworks. In the early 1970s, PICO, formerly the Pacific Institute for Community Organizing, began with secular, neighbourhood organizing in Oakland and recognizing the strength of church-based groups quickly evolved a faith-based model to engage a relatively diverse sampling of faith communities in the political process, especially Catholic, Protestant and Unitarian Universalist churches, Reform synagogues, and more recently, mosques, and secular non-profits (cf., Wood 2002).

While the 1980s and 1990s are often characterized as being a time of declining political participation, polarizing suburban/conurbanization, disorganized urban dissent (e.g., the 1992 Los Angeles riots), and disempowerment, the charge that this form of organizing is simply issue-based and local, overlooks the sustained energy and powerful relationships that specific victories during this period symbolize. For instance, when SDOP responded to the needs of its own membership, which included undocumented immigrants vulnerable to INS threats and upper middle class families whose grown children could not afford to stay in the region, they seized a political opportunity and commissioned a policy study that demonstrated how city ordinances regarding rents, rental agreements and evictions, in combination with the high cost of housing for workers and families adversely were affecting all sectors. In 2002, the City Council declared a housing state of emergency thus opening the door to many more housing-related gains for SDOP and galvanizing a transcommunal, cross-class alliance including empowered community members, city officials and coalitions across various sectors.

While my focus here is neither how religion serves as an undercurrent in political life, nor simply grassroots organizing among churches, a structural-historical perspective of organizing in the U.S. acknowledges that churches and other faith-based communities have been instrumental in challenging the broader society to confront the contradictions of democratic ideals with the social and economic realities lived by workers, the poor, and people of colour expressly by invoking social justice values. As I prepare to look closely at the organizing model used by PICO and emulated by a host of other U.S. organizations, large and small, I raise for discussion the challenge, which organizing frameworks offer to engaged ethnographic practices: Specifically, organizing frameworks require reciprocal relations of accountability from all participants in a process, which connects empathetic listening to direct action supported by research. My argument is that the best critiques of anthropology as a social science discipline similarly point up the possibility of producing ethnographic inquiry that reflects the needs of the communities with whom we research, suggest specific courses of action that we can take in solidarity with activists; and require accountable relationships throughout a process that does not end with research. Specific points of convergence with engaged anthropology, then, include the emphasis of organizing on the concerns of the people with whom we work, a definition of power that attends to the structural constraints on human behaviour, or, phrased differently, a critique of power that seeks to advance and redistribute knowledge about the rules of the political, social and cultural systems in which people can act on their own behalf, both individually and collectively. In what follows, I propose that we can read and work across these domains of power/knowledge production.

Here I turn to a close look at the organizing model and key principles, glossed as "the PICO process," and I relate the latter to the steps for conducting respectful research that engages the radical critique of Western social science as thoughtfully elaborated by Charles Menzies in his work as a Native anthropologist among Indigenous peoples (2001; see also 2004). These closing arguments, then, seek to demonstrate how the primary aims in organizing (the surfacing of issues to be addressed through collective action) overlap with the objectives (and, consequently, values) of engaged research, which is to create knowledge that serves the community.

The PICO Process: "Power Is a Product of Relationships"

While the PICO organizing model can be simplified to five irreducible steps, paid organizers and community members, who are willing to commit to leadership roles for any length of time, receive rigorous local, state and national training on how to develop a shared understanding of the process within the local organizing committee (a.k.a. an "LOC"). Among the tools organizers and leaders accrue are various trainings that break down the model even further, and they practice employing nearly fifty "principles" that illustrate various aspects of the logic behind the process. When for instance, one says that "organizing is about people, and people are about issues," she reminds herself and others that the work of surfacing issues to be acted upon should never come before an interest in the person. A second principle further elucidates this PICO orientation: "power is a product of relationships." Thus, building the organization is necessary to mobilize the LOC to take collective action, but the strength of collective action lies in people acting out of their own self-interest, which over time broadens to encompass the concerns they share with others. A third principle that synopsizes the entire process is "push on a problem you get issues; push on an issue, you get values." In addition to locating the need to push people to see that injustice contradicts both faith values and democratic values, this statement implies the thrust of the organizing: when people have the opportunity to express their problems and are heard by someone who shares these concerns, they build relationships with other members of the LOC, and sometimes they are ready to take the next steps, which are defining the issue and mobilizing collective action. When organizers summarize the PICO process, they often use the following flowchart:

1-1's – Research – Action – Reflection – 1-1's

Despite its apparent simplicity, the process of moving an entire congregation to action and beyond can be a long one. Aptly, then, the first and the last step in the PICO process is to listen, using the "one-to-one interview" (hereafter rendered in the organization's nomenclature, "1-1"). By focusing on the PICO process and the methods of anthropology, this article avoids using the personal content of individual 1-1's conducted with community members. Instead I focus on the significance of the interview in the production of power/knowledge. Specifically, I use interviews with organizing directors, the PICO training manual (see references), my training notes from 2003 to 2005, and published literature to draw out the overlap and potential interplay between approaches. Similar to the process for mobilizing social action, Menzies outlines four basic steps for a methodological approach to "respectful research relations" drawn from his experience as a consultant commissioned by First Nations as well as in the capacity of independent researcher (2001:21). In brief, these include initiating dialogue, refining the research plan, conducting the research, and finally, writing, analysis, revision and distribution (22). In his analysis, the primary principle of engaged anthropological approaches should be to resist expanding "the knowledge and power of the dominant society at the expense of the colonized and the excluded," and he underscores the importance of remaining in contact with the community in the following way: "Whenever possible, meetings should be held to discuss and analyze research results. ... The ultimate aim is to democratize access to specialized research skills and research as much as possible so that research can by conducted in the community and by the community and/or complement the research already underway in the community" (22). This approach of using direct communication and equipping the people with whom we work to conduct research articulates with the commitments of organizers and leaders to use 1-1's throughout the process and the explicit aim of organizing to recruit, support and train community leaders as they develop their own capacities as empowered agents of social change.

1-1's: Listening, Talking and Testifying

1-1's are seen as the "foundation" of people-centered organizing, because they are used in every stage of the process to sharpen or regain focus and to build relationships. Specifically, 1-1's are structured half-hour interviews with individual church members who have expressed interest in addressing a specific issue or want to learn more about organizing in their community. Conducted as house-visits or meetings at a local coffee shop by organizers, and sometimes by members of the local organizing committee who are participating in a "listening campaign," 1-1's are vital to the PICO process because they give people an opportunity to express their dreams, hopes, and concerns about where they live; to be heard by someone who cares; and to be introduced to the aims and accountabilities of organizing. Organizing seeks to more than merely elicit a personalized description of a problem; rather as part of the process, the interview begins to ask people to see how their problems impact the entire community and offers the opportunity to take responsibility to make systemic change as part of a collective. Thus, these interviews begin the process by identifying problems that can be framed as issues to be acted upon, and initiating the relationships that establish power for the organization – that is, those between the organizer and the individual, between the individual and the organizing committee, and between the LOC and the broader society.

Research Is the Bridge

According to PICO, "research is the bridge that takes us across problems to issues," and as the process flowchart illustrates research traverses the expanse from listening to action. Expressed more evocatively by a lead organizer in San Diego, cutting an actionable issue is "like slicing a loaf of bread." Whereas a problem, such as poverty, is general, vague, often overwhelming and indigestible, an issue, on the other hand is specific, identifying who is affected, who is responsible, who can do something, and which discrete steps can bring about change. PICO research then is a collective process, where LOC members meet with each other and think together about how to personalize and polarize problems into issues. Personalizing a problem is crucial, because problems are specific to real people, thus building the power to make change requires relationships among specific persons. Polarizing the issue, on the other hand, clarifies what should be done – for instance, noticing that city allocations pay for sidewalks in La Jolla, and not in the barrio – frames the problem as a "winnable" issue, invoking fairness and justice. At this stage, members of the LOC may also meet with officials who may be aware of these issues, know about some of the challenges, and share a common policy agenda. Again, 1-1's within the LOC are vital to this step in the process, because they identify the relationships to be drawn upon during the action; that is, the resulting action connects the person who experiences the problem to others with similar experience and to the public officials who are responsible and have the authority to make change.

Action: Pushing the Issues

In PICO-speak, "an issue is a problem we can act upon," so all of the steps of organizing channel problems and pursue action. Actions, or public events, usually occur at the LOC's home church and typically involve publicly confronting public officials with the power to make change, "pinning them" to acknowledging their responsibility, and asking them to commit to taking a concrete step to create change. Here, 1-1's are instrumental to the identification of people who are willing to speak out and to their preparation of testimonies that powerfully illustrate the issue and effectively describe an attainable policy change. When sharing their testimonies, LOC members simultaneously demonstrate to members of the church that their voices (and numbers) matter and to public officials that a valuable constituency both demands change and supports them in addressing community problems. Thus, in the long term, actions "get results" in terms of the policy change and services that low-income communities need, but in the shorter term, actions create situations where community members demonstrate discipline (as is implied in the word "organization"), and exercise and build power. To repeat in PICO language: "power is a product of relationships," so actions forge and strengthen relationships in the LOC, between the LOC and the broader community, and between the community and public officials.

Conclusion: Are Organizing Models Consistent with Methodologies for Engaged Anthropology?

Of course, the PICO process (or model) has many facets that I leave unexplored here, but as the flowchart demonstrated, the process returns to its beginning and represents a cycle, recognizing that issues and interests shift, but people and relationships among them endure. Ideally, the process never ends. Abbreviating the key principle for momentary emphasis to "organizing is about people," one might observe that anthropology is also about people, and that engaged anthropology, too, considers the concerns of people with whom we conduct research to be of critical importance. I have argued that if the purpose of research in organizing is to understand "what could be versus the reality of what is," and "what we can do to change it," then the aims of engaged anthropological research might be understood similarly. What does engaged anthropology as such call us to do or be? Who is activist research for? What contribution does it make? If anthropologists concur with organizers that power is indeed a product of relationships, which ethnographic methods or practices support the relationships that demand, support and facilitate positive social change?

In the PICO model, the structured interview is not a one-on-one, but a "one to one," establishing that "relationships are reciprocal," quid pro quo. The interview, then, offers more than merely a method for gathering information and a process for handling testimonies; rather it channels the information through three main exchanges, listening, empathy, and challenge. All of these interactions interpellate both speaker and listener into a two-way relationship. I suggest that decolonized, ethnographic inquiry offers similar opportunities. The challenge from an organizing perspective is when the questions move from listening and actively hearing to confronting rationalizations and contradictions: Why do you think this problem exists; why don't people get involved; and what have you done or not; and why? These questions suggest that there might be a solution, that responsibility rests somewhere specific, and that all parties could work together to act. The PICO model proposes that "challenge involves risk" and "creates tension." The challenge to the anthropologist who is called to action, then, is: are you ready to be in relationship, to be with people where they are at, and to walk them on their journey? And if not, why?

I have attempted to address this last question by reflecting on and interrogating my own role and practice as an apprentice, anthropologist, and organizer in Guatemala and the U.S. In this reflection on the interplay between organizing models and respectful approaches to engaged anthropology, I have attempted to contextualize ongoing disciplinary attempts to decolonize social science paradigms alongside and within shared activist trajectories and to examine how the desires and intentions of researchers seeking to contribute to social change might shift to situate researchers in solidarity (a powerful relationship) with activists and organizers by simultaneously employing respectful, engaged methodological approaches, socially and historically-contextualizing our shared trajectories, and acknowledging values as potentially more useful than an ideology that leaves the anthropologist as an ineffectual, objective outsider.

Acknowledgements

I thank the members of the San Diego Organizing Project and of PICO National for granting the interviews I used to think through this paper; however, I take full responsibility for the conclusions drawn in this paper and for any errors. (I have attempted to attribute with accuracy various principles and statements to the PICO organization, but it should be noted that the 200, unnumbered pages of the training manual comprise a living text in a state of constant revision, which may have changed somewhat since 2003.) I also thank the members of the Garifuna community in Livingston, Guatemala for pushing me to continue building my own critique of anthropology and toolkit for participation in collective action that pursues progressive social change. Finally, I express sincere gratitude to the Department of Anthropology at the University of South Carolina, Columbia for partially funding my trip to the meetings where I presented an early draft of this paper; to Dr. Adriana D.M. Briscoe for practical support; and to A.E. Kingsolver for ongoing intellectual support, exceeding her responsibilities as a mentor, and indeed modelling engaged, activist teaching.

References

Abu-Lughod, Lila
1990   Can There be a Feminist Ethnography? *In* Women and Performance: A Journal of Feminist Theory 5(1):7–27.
1991   Writing against Culture. *In* Recapturing Anthropology: Working in the Present. Richard Fox, ed. Santa Fe, NM: School of American Research Press.
Alexander, M. Jacqui and Chandra Talpade Mohanty,
1997   Introduction : Genealogies, Legacies, Movements. *In* Feminist Genealogies, Colonial Legacies, Democratic Futures. Pp. xii-xlii. New York: Routledge.
Alinsky, Saul D.
1971   Rules for Radicals: A Practical Primer for Realistic Radicals. New York: Random House.
Alvarez, Sonia E.
1998   The NGOization of Latin American Feminisms. *In* Cultures of Politics/ Politics of Cultures: Re-Visioning Latin American Social Movements. Sonia E. Alvarez, Evelina Dagnino, and Arturo Escobar, eds. Pp 306-324. Boulder, CO.: Westview Press.

Boggs, Carl
1997   The Great Retreat: Decline of the Public Sphere in Late Twentieth-Century America. Theory and Society 26(6). December:741-780.

Braude, Ann
2004   A Religious Feminist Who Can Find Her? Historiographical Challenges from the National Organization for Women. The Journal of Religion October, Vol. 84(4):513-513.

Eckstein, Susan, ed.
2001   Power and Popular Protest: Latin American Social Movements. Berkeley: University of California Publishing.

Escobar, Arturo
1995   Encountering Development: The Making and Unmaking of the Third World. Princeton: Princeton University Press.

Higginbotham, Evelyn Brooks
1996   Religion, Politics, and Gender: The Leadership of Nannie Helen Burroughs. *In* This Far by Faith: Readings in African-American Women's Religious Biography. Judith Weisenfeld and Richard Newman, eds. New York: Routledge Press.
1993   Righteous Discontent: The Women's Movement in Black Baptist Church 1880-1920. Cambridge, MA.: Harvard University Press.

Hope, Anne and Sally Timmel
1999   Training for Transformation: A Handbook for Community Workers. UK: ITDG Publishing.

Hymes, Dell, ed.
1969   Reinventing Anthropology. New York: Pantheon.

Marcus, George E. and Michael F. Fisher
1986   Anthropology as Cultural Critique: An Experimental Moment in the Human Sciences. Chicago: University of Chicago Press.

Meier, Deborah
1995   The Power of Their Ideas: Lessons for America from a Small School in Harlem. Boston: Beacon Press.

Menzies, Charles R.
2004   Putting Words into Action: Negotiating Collaborative Research in Gitxaała. Canadian Journal of Native Education 28(1&2). 2004.
2001   Reflections on Research with, for, and among Indigenous Peoples. Canadian Journal of Native Education. 25(1):19-36.

PICO (The Pacific Institute for Community Organizing)

    2003   Training Manual. (Unpublished.)

Rosaldo, Renato

    1989   Culture and Truth: The Remaking of Social Analysis. Boston: Beacon Press.

Said, Edward

    1996   Representations of the Intellectual. New York: Vintage Books.

Skocpol, Theda, Marshall Ganz, and Ziad Munson

    2000   A Nation of Organizers: The Institutional Origins of Civic Voluntarism in the United States. The American Political Science Review. 94(3):527-546.

Whitman, Gordon

    2006   Beyond Advocacy: The History & Vision of the PICO Network. Social Policy. Winter 2006-2007:50-59.

Wood, Richard L.

    2007   Higher Power: Strategic Capacity for State and National Organizing. *In* Transforming the City: Community Organizing and the Challenge of Political Change. Marion Orr, ed. Lawrence, Kansas: University Press of Kansas.

    2002   Faith in Action: Religion, Race, and Democratic Organizing in America. Chicago: University of Chicago Press.

Zavella, Patricia

    1997   Feminist Insider Dilemmas: Constructing Ethnic Identity with Chicana Informants. *In* Situated Lives, Gender and Culture in Everyday Life. L. Lamphere, H. Ragone, and P. Zavella, eds. New York: Routledge.

Reflections on Work and Activism in the 'University of Excellence'

Charles R. Menzies

The University, through its students, faculty, staff, and alumni, strives for excellence and educates students to the highest standards. Place and Promise: The UBC Plan

Excellence has the singular advantage of being entirely meaningless. Bill Readings, *The University in Ruin.*

Excellence is the goal contemporary society strives for: excellence in sport, in business, in art, in scholarship, and in life in general. Yet as Bill Readings so pointedly observes, contemporary society has emptied the idea of 'excellence' of meaning. The search for excellence structures workplace competition, student recruitment, and the evaluation of practically all aspects of the contemporary university environment. In its operational mode excellence is little more than a set of quantified indictors – dollar value of grants, number of publications, ranking of publication venue, completion rates of students, and so on. These indicators are tabulated by individual, unit, or university and then ranked accordingly. Deriving from the tautological market principle that those who win are by definition excellent, being top ranked makes one excellent. There is, however, a problem if too many people get the reward. The crux of excellence is its reliance upon failure as the foil against which it is itself determined. Excellence is no absolute; it's a normative measure that relies on failure and the threat of failure to propel people to engage in acts of self-exploitation simply to keep their employment or their place in the university of excellence.

It is critical to note that this is not an argument for incompetence, an excuse for inadequacy, nor a call for the mediocre. My focus is on the way that excellence as a concept (not as a quality) is tied into the ideology of neo-liberal capitalism. Capitalism in general is a system by which mechanisms of a free market are used to regulate and control human transactions and engagements. There are obviously historically contingent and regional variants of capitalism. What I ask the reader to focus on is the way in which excellence has become a core term for a series of labour management practices that have insinuated themselves into the belief system of academic labourers. The power of the neo-liberal concept of excellence is that it presents as a quality academics all aspire to while simultaneously undermining the possibility of actually obtaining it. Our work becomes measured by quantity and placement of output: "so long as one publishes with the prestigious academic presses and journals, one's publications are 'excellent'" (Wang 2005:535). The paradox is that we become embedded within the hegemonic discourse as we attempt to labour within the context of our workplace: we are, in a manner of speaking, damned if we do, damned if we don't.

This paper is an autoethnography of the university of excellence. That is, I draw from my personal experience as a student and then professor within a series of North American universities. In this paper I reflect on three linked, but autonomous, social moments within my scholarly career: 'On Strike!' a story of student radicalism; 'In Struggle!' a story about academic labour, and; 'New Proposals (Again!),' a manifesto for action.[1] Each of these moments revolves around a particular aspect of the university of excellence, its structure and location within the wider society, and the ways in which engaged progressive political action might intersect with the realities of our everyday work and lives.

On Strike!

The social space of 'student' provides – at least in theory – the opportunity and capacity to act that one appears to lose when enmeshed within mainstream employment and respectable middle age. It is a social space that gives license to radical, anti-social, or experimental behaviours and perspectives (see, for example: Pfaff 2009). This notion is well captured in that famous old saw: "If you aren't a socialist in your youth you have no heart. But, if you're still a socialist in middle age you have no brains."

---

1   These sections were original presented as a part of a trilogy of papers at the annual meetings of the Canadian Anthropology Society (CASCA).

The student social space is facilitated by our society's extended notion of late childhood; that is, the social categories of teenager and youth. This makes an engagement with alternative futures possible while simultaneously diminishing their importance through a folk model in which such experiments are discounted as the 'antics' of youth. It is not, however, a space of total freedom. Possibilities are constrained by historical facts, cultural forces, and the general structures within which people finds themselves. Yet it is this very possibility of change and innovation that gives power to student protest movements. As a faculty member within the university of excellence I see contemporary students struggle with the possibility of political activism within a context that has changed significantly since my own days as a student activist.

The memories of the earlier generation of the 1960s and 1970s student radicals overshadowed my own student radicalism in the 1980s. Their stories of struggle made it sound as though it had all been done before. Yet, as is often the case with youth, our optimism and excitement in the face of what was new to us propelled us forward. In my circle we found Rosa Luxemburg's idea of spontaneous struggle and the mass strike beguiling even as we overlooked the importance she placed on organization and the historical moment. Nonetheless, we saw this as a means to organize and advance in the face of a deepening attack against public education and an emerging agenda that later became familiar to us as neo-liberalism.

The universities of the 1980s were in the early phases of the new corporate university of excellence (Readings 1996).[2] They were still partly in recovery from the protests of the 1970s, but they were also striding forward with new forms of privatization and techniques of labour control. Universities followed industry with the establishment of two-tiered contracts for academic labourers: one set of rules for tenure-stream/tenured faculty; a much less rewarding set for a growing body of part-timers (Patterson 2001). At the same time tuition fees and class sizes exploded across North America. The radical call to make university scholarship meaningful was degraded into a less progressive utilitarianism linked to notions of economic efficiency and job training. This is the moment within which I entered into student politics.

I came to university having grown up in Prince Rupert, a northern British Columbia resource dependent community, where strikes and labour conflict had

---

2   This is not to say that universities have ever been anything more than a central part of the ideological apparatus of capitalist societies. However, there have been a series of forms, the corporate university of excellence being only the most recent.

been the normative backdrop against which one learned about the world. Born in the early 1960s, I am perched at the end of the baby boom and the beginning of what fellow BCer and author Douglas Coupland (1991) called "Generation X." My political coming of age was formed in the shadows of *les enfants soixante-huit*.[3] Though I vaguely recall the 1967 centennial 'Canada song'[4] from TV commercials it is the shocked tones of family conversations and the accompanying harsh black and white news reels of the declaration of martial law by Canadian Prime Minister Pierre Elliot Trudeau in October 1970[5] and the Kent State killings[6] that brought the wider world to my attention. And, while I do recall joining my cousins in their TV room to watch the first moon landing in 1969, it was the fall of Saigon[7] in 1975 that resonates most strongly in my memory.

These global events played in the background in my hometown but also set the stage for the material conditions of the everyday. We too had our own crises and conflicts. The 1970s was the turning point of the long post war economic boom. High interest rates and low rates of growth combined with a growing resistance on the part of capital to working class demands; these were the conditions out of which the neo-liberal assault began.[8] By the 1980s the 'new right' was in full swing and privatization, retrenchment, and debt reduction became the language of the day.

---

3   The 'children of 1968,' as the generation of protest came to be called in France.

4   Canada song http://www.youtube.com/ watch?v=lE0nhnwNcgU

5   The 1970 October Crisis was Canada's late 20th century experience with radical left politics and radical Québécois nationalism. Early in October 1970 James Cross, British Trade Commission in Montreal, was kidnapped by the *Front de libération du Québec* (FLQ). A few days later Quebec Labour Minister Pierre Laporte was kidnapped by the FLQ. In response the federal government invoked the War Measures Act (WMA), the first time in Canadian history during peacetime, which led to a military occupation of Montreal. The WMA suspended civil liberties and allowed for the arrest without charge of several hundred political activists in Montreal and across Canada. James Cross survived his kidnapping, but Laporte was summarily executed by strangulation.

6   The Kent State University shootings occurred in the context of a student protest against the U.S. invasion of Cambodia. Members of the Ohio National Guard who were policing the demonstration killed four students and wounded nine others in a 13 second barrage of bullets. Over the course of the previous three days escalating student protests had lead to the conservative university administration, acting with the State government, to call in the National Guard. However, the very fact that the students were unarmed and that several of the dead had not even been involved in the protest fueled American and world-wide opposition outrage. The Kent State shootings became a pivotal event in the anti-war movement of the 1970s.

7   Saigon was the capital of South Vietnam and the base of U.S. military operations during the Vietnam war. In April 1975 the U.S. were finally pushed out of Vietnam. U.S. citizens and supporters were evacuated by helicopter. Striking images of people rushing the gates of the U.S. embassy as overloaded helicopters, some with people barely able to hold on, flooded world news programs. It was a humiliating defeat for the world's then leading super-power. But it was also a powerful and jubilant event for many who opposed the war and who saw in the U.S. occupation of Vietnam a blatant act of imperialist aggression.

8   In Prince Rupert labour strife was a strong component of the 1970s. I have written about one aspect of this struggle within the local fishing industry (Menzies 1990, 1992, 2001b).

Back in my hometown the rising cost of resource extractive industries – in terms of capital investment requirements and environmental impacts – was progressively undermining the local economy. Working class struggles were increasingly on the defensive. From a working class point of view the demands of green activists was seen as yet another form of middle class dilettantism and meddling. The strengthening movement and legal support for indigenous title and rights claims was increasingly supported by capital while simultaneously being experienced as prejudicial by the non-indigenous members of the working and petty bourgeois classes (Menzies 1994). This experience of working class and indigenous struggle provided the context for my engagement in the university as a student.

The universities I attended in the 1980s and early 1990s were in the throes of the neo-liberal transition. The idea of education as a right was being replaced by a concept of education as a commodity to purchase. Measures of economic efficiency were being applied with increasing rigour in the face of budgetary cutbacks from government funding agencies. The following two stories of student activism occurred in the context of the emergence of the university of excellence and the imposition of a neo-liberal agenda.

Solidarity Coalition

Following their election in May of 1983, Premier Bill Bennett and his Social Credit Party proclaimed a 'new reality' had arrived for British Columbia.[9] The provincial government immediately began a radical transformation of provincial services and programs in a series of actions that was to foreshadow the next three decades of provincial politics in BC. Under the 'new reality' six thousand provincial employees were to be laid off, the labour code was to be revised in favour of business, and social service, healthcare and education programs and budgets were to be cut (Carroll and Ratner 1989; Palmer 1987; Quine 1985; Ratner 1998:110-112). Despite a growing opposition in the streets and loud opposition in the legislative assembly, the passage of an omnibus package of legislation seemed to be progressing without serious challenge. It is from this political moment that the Solidarity Coalition (a broad-based

---

9   The Social Credit Party in B.C. had its roots in a depression era political theory. The theory behind 'social credit' was the notion that the depression was caused by a lack of disposable income. This gave rise to the famous A + B = C theorem. That is, money in people's hands (A) leads them to spend (B) which combine to drive the economy (C). The practical application of this was for the government to give people money to spend. By the time Bill Bennett was elected Premier in 1983 the party was on the vanguard of the neo-liberal agenda. The party was also a dynasty that Bill Bennett inherited from his father who had formed the first Social Credit Party in B.C. in 1952 and, with a three year exception in the 1970s, it was the governing party of British Columbia until its scandal-ridden collapse in 1991.

alliance of community groups and labour organizations) and Operation Solidarity (the trade union wing of the protest movement) was formed. As the summer progressed to autumn, the protest movement ramped up to a full-blown province-wide public sector strike that threatened to spread into the private sector industrial unions.

As an undergraduate student and student politician at Simon Fraser University (SFU) in the early 1980s, I was actively involved in a grassroots network of students whose political links were closely tied to extra-parliamentary leftist groups such as Socialist Challenge, International Socialists, The Revolutionary Workers League, elements of the New Democratic Party and the now defunct Workers Communist Party – an intriguing and complex alliance of divergent left groups, most of whom had their genesis in 1960s New Left politics. There were of course other elements involved and the emergence of postmodern lifestyle politics were already evident in our organizing meetings.

As student activists we saw the growing Operation Solidarity/Solidarity Coalition as an opportunity to shift the balance of power from the top-down unionism of the day to a grassroots organized mass movement that might actually topple the government. Thus we joined with the 'prepare the general strike' committee, a left faction of the trade union movement that was gaining grassroots support from wood and mill workers in the metropolitan Vancouver region and in the interior of the province. For the first time in more than a decade, the Simon Fraser Student Society called a special general meeting of the student body that achieved quorum (over 500 people). We voted to join the strike.

From our point of view as student activists we drew upon the strength and public legitimacy of the Solidarity Coalition in advocating within our classrooms prior to the walk out, and then in organizing our picket line work where we actively stopped cars, busses, and pedestrians from entering campus. We entered into the area of conflict partly out of the excitement of the moment and partly out of a belief that through this action things could be made better. Perhaps we could have made a real difference had the more conservative union movement leadership not lost their nerve. Clearly, leadership does make a difference and in the absence of a coordinated political organization outside of the social democratic power structure of the NDP and the BC Federation of Labour it was not possible to shift the narrow economism of the union establishment. From within the centre of student activism and protest we understood the possibility of progressive change even if we lacked the real political reach to make it happen. The university of excellence, as one of the cornerstones of the neo-liberal agenda, was triumphant. There was a general understanding of the criticalness of the political juncture but the established progressive and union leadership didn't seem to realize the long term implications of the loss.

CUNY Strike

The City University of New York is a venerable public institution consisting of 23 separate campuses including the Graduate School and University Center, senior colleges such as City College, Hunter, Lehman, Queens, and junior colleges which – at least in principle – are designed to meet the higher educational needs of the residents of New York City. For decades CUNY has been a key focal point of assimilation and integration of aspiring entrants to the growing 20th century middle class.

Widespread community-based struggles in the 1960s and 1970s created new openings for students of working class, minority, and immigrant roots. Two key issues helped establish this entrée: an open admissions policy that undermined the restrictions created by class privilege and a tuition policy that kept the cost of access relatively low compared to other public universities and colleges (in fact tuition had been free for over 100 years). Most of these gains have now been undermined by New York State's own brand of neo-liberalism. Open admissions has effectively been removed by the cutting of all upgrading courses, persistent funding cuts, and the arrival of standards of 'excellence.' The same global issues that were instrumental in sparking the Solidarity Coalition of 1983 in B.C. also set the stage for the CUNY strike of 1991.

The attacks against public institutions in New York throughout the 1980s and 1990s were part of a more general attack against the public provision of social services, education, and health. University administrators were trying to meet funding shortfalls through increased tuition, restrictive admissions policies, and the undermining of educational services in general. Governments were interested in privatizing and divesting themselves of costly social services such as public education. Market mechanisms were becoming the flavour of the day.

My involvement in the CUNY Strike began in 1990 as a new doctoral student and occurred in the context of the first Bush war against the mideast. One of my friends recently reminded me that during that fall we ran a poster featuring pictures of Mario Cuomo, then Governor of New York, W. Ann Renolds, Chancellor of CUNY, and the late Saddam Hussein, the former president of Iraq. Under their pictures our caption read: "Who is the real enemy?" We were facing a massive increase in tuition fees and a nearly debilitating budget cut. From this perspective, the representatives of political elites in the U.S. seemed far more of a threat than any distant political leader.[10]

The CUNY strike was system wide. Spurred into action by student activists at the City College of the City University of New York (CCNY), groups of students began taking over their campuses throughout the CUNY system. By the end of the occupation more than two-thirds of CUNY was under student occupation. At the Graduate Center we organized an action in support of the CUNY colleges. Our core group of a dozen or so people was comprised primarily of anthropology students. We shared a common socialist political orientation that informed our approach to organization. Whereas the CCNY students used a cadre-type system in which only those directly involved could participate in decision-making, we opted for a participatory model of democracy. Thus, as our occupation proceeded we held a vote each day on whether to continue or end our occupation. With a process and plan in hand, we took action several days after CCNY students took over their campus with the idea of holding our campus in support of the other striking CUNY students.

In the early 1990s the CUNY Graduate School and University Center occupied an 18-story office tower in mid-town Manhattan, just across the street from the research centre of the New York Public Library and Bryant Park. The ground level of the building had an open mall that connected 41st and 42nd Streets with a public walkway. Overnight a set of security gates were lowered to close off the mall, but normally these gates would have been up by the time of the planned takeover. In previous years' occupations, students had simply taken over the public mall and that had been our intention. However, when we arrived the security gates were down. Our symbolic takeover of the public mall became a real occupation of the entire building.

We had to show our student identification to enter the building past the security gates and into a lobby by the main bank of elevators. Once our first small group was in we asked the security guards standing there to leave the building. "This is a student occupation. We are in control of the building now," we told them. All but one of the guards agreed to leave. Later that morning one of the student occupiers forcefully

---

10   And, as history has shown us, the threat of Iraq was more myth than reality. In the first Bush war the Iraqi Army essentially dissolved under the assault of American aerial bombardment and ground assault. Many of the horror stories of Iraqi atrocities (such as the infamous baby incubator hoax) turned out to be false. The real atrocity was the thousands of ill-equipped Iraqis burned and bombed as they fled Kuwait City. The second Bush war, initiated in response to the claims that Iraq held weapons of mass destruction, has also proven to be based on a falsehood – there were no weapons of mass destruction. In the wake of a decade of warfare Iraq seems ungovernable; a country in turmoil that is now, more than ever before, likely to spawn America's much feared Islamic Terrorists.

expelled the remaining guard. Once we had the building firmly under control, we called in other students who had been waiting nearby.

Our guiding principles were those of radical participatory democracy. In practice this meant that we held a public open air meeting each day of the occupation. Anyone who wanted could vote on whether or not to continue the occupation. Inside the occupation we also had meetings to discuss how things were going, draft and approve public statements, and to consider the position to put forward in the following day's open air meeting. Our notion of radical democratic practice emerged out of our particular idea of radical socialism and our critique of anti-democratic variations of socialism and mainstream politics in which dissent and diversity are suppressed in favour of a so-called common good. We were motivated by the ideal of participatory democracy encoded in the twin concepts of trust and risk. That is, for democracy to work one must place trust in people to be fully engaged; but also, we must be willing to take the risk that things will not work out as one hopes.

We started our occupation as a consciously symbolic act. That is, we realized that simply taking over a piece of real estate had no independent value or meaning outside of the wider context of struggle. The Graduate Center occupied a position of prestige within the CUNY system, but it was not a center of power. The power of our action was as an act of solidarity with students at colleges like Bronx, CCNY, Hostos, Hunter, Lehman, or Queens where the majority of New York students attended. Yet, as the occupation progressed the perspective of the participants shifted toward what I came to call a militant liberal perspective in which the physical control of the building became the central issue. As the occupation deepened, the students who joined us came more and more to feel that controlling the graduate centre building meant that we had control of real power and lost sight of the wider context within which our actions existed.

The militant liberals – students who were part of the then popular post-modernist academic movement – argued that holding control over the building was in and of itself sufficient to cause the university to negotiate with us and to meet our demands for a tuition freeze. Those of us who had organized the occupation argued that our only power lay in our ability to extend our struggle beyond the building and to forge real political linkages with local trade union and community movements such as we saw represented in the college-based struggles. With the lesson of the soviet failure to build 'socialism in one country'[11] we rejected the idea that a group of elite outsiders (most of us at the graduate centre were out-of-state students) could build a progressive movement in one office tower. Eventually a compromise was reached that allowed us to hand over the building to the administration while holding on to some modest political gains.

The militant liberalism that emerged in the course of the CUNY strike at the graduate center has its echo in the radical posturing of small 'l' liberal academics who publish biting critiques of the powers that be but do nothing in their own workplaces or home communities. This is a politics that denies the reality of political struggle and instead fetishizes radical text and clever theory. It is also a form of academic politics that reveals the extent to which working classes have been forced into retreat (Callinicos 1990). While the power of B.C.'s working class in 1983 was still sufficient to mount a major defensive struggle, by the 1990s the capacity of New York's working class movement was fractured by race, ethnicity, and the debilitating effects of the American neo-liberal agenda.

In Context

The Solidarity Coalition and the CUNY student strike were both situated within particular local contexts. However, they were also local responses to wider global processes in which those in charge of the global capitalist system were attempting to shift the balance of power back toward capital. During the long post-war boom that created the conditions for the so-called affluent society (Galbraith 1998) working class people had managed – at least in the western economies – to push their standard of living to levels not previously seen. Facing the threat of workers winning more than better wages, western ruling classes entered into an historic compromise with labour (Przeworski 1985). As conditions changed over the course of the post-war decades this compromise became less tenable to the ruling classes and the compromise broke apart – hence the rise of the neo-liberal agenda.

Operation Solidarity/Solidarity Coalition was part of a broad-based social moment that linked trade unions, political parties and community groups. Other

---

11 'Socialism in one country' refers to the Stalinist idea that it was possible to create the conditions of a classless society by turning inward and in ignoring the world around. However, this is not in fact possible and, in the Soviet case, led to horrendous atrocities and loss of life and ultimately created a state capitalist regime that shared with the west a form of corporatist control over labour through a managerial class. At the core of the socialist argument is that revolution may well start in one country but that the path toward a true communist society requires the constant expansion of the revolution outward until all vestiges of capitalism are eradicated. Stalin's approach was initially made out of necessity in the face of revolutionary defeat but it ultimately became a rationalization for the autarkic authoritarianism of Stalin's USSR.

examples of the solidarity coalition can be found in the mid 1990s struggles against the neo-liberal government of Ontario,[12] and in the weaker protests against the neo-liberal government of Gordon Campbell in B.C. since 2001.[13] What sets the Solidarity Coalition apart is that it marks the end of a long wave of working class resurgence in British Columbia. The Socred attacks were part of the opening salvo of neo-liberalism in North America.

The CUNY strike of 1991 represented the end point of a similar movement or period of social advance and prefigured the political transformations of neo-liberalism within public post-secondary education in New York State. But in New York issues of race and ethnicity heavily overwrote the dynamics of the struggle. Whereas the State University of New York (SUNY) was predominantly white, the CUNY system was predominantly Latino and African-American. The roll back of

12   Though many commentators locate the origins of the neo-liberal agenda in Ontario with the 'common sense revolution' of Mike Harris and his conservative government (1995-2002) it was in fact under the social democratic (New Democratic Party or NDP) government of Bob Rae (1990-1995) that neo-liberalism was applied in its classic sense in Ontario. The NDP has been the traditional party of the Keynesian compromise in Canada. The party has attempted to govern, when it has been in power, through a combination of ad hoc social policy spending (i.e. housing, healthcare, education) combined with middle of the road economic policy that maintains the rule of capital. This form of happy-face capitalism seems to work in periods of economic growth. However, when capitalism is in crisis social democratic governments have lacked the stomach to take over the commanding heights of the economy and have instead retreated into fiscal policies that are indistinguishable from mainstream pro-enterprise parties. Rae retreated from his social democratic roots made in 1993 after he watched a CTV news documentary on the fiscal crisis in New Zealand (Crow 1999:184). Fearing that only a radical neo-liberal approach could 'save' Ontario from economic disaster Rae compelled his caucus colleagues to introduce a new 'social contract' that froze public sector wages, opened and rewrote collective agreements (something that would happen again in BC following the election of the Gordon Campbell BC Liberal government), and enforced mandatory days off without pay (which came to be called "Rae-Days" by disgruntled workers). Wage rollbacks were coupled by an austerity budget that slashed public sector spending. Rae's economic policy turnaround ushered in a decade of social cuts and deterioration in public services, the ramifications of which are still being felt in Ontario today.

13   Gordon Campbell's provincial BC Liberal Party was elected in May 2001. The Liberals defeated a discredited ten-year old New Democratic party government. Under the BC NDP the provincial government had tried to walk the line between fiscal restraint and targeted social project spending. Despite this, the general direction of the NDP's fiscal policy was aligned with that of Bob Rae's Ontario NDP government. The Campbell innovation was to come in hard with a massive series of fiscal cutbacks, government restructuring, privatization of core government business and services, and to legislate new collective agreements across the public sector. Where the NDP had vacillated between cozying up to business and demanding support from their traditional supporters in labour, the Liberals had no such problems and systematically removed from appointed office all those not directly supportive of their political agenda. In the university sector this can be seen in the face of government appointees to Boards of Governors. In the early years of the Campbell government the trade union movement tried to rally support. Aside from a few showcase rallies on the grounds of the provincial legislature and sporadic protests from parents, teachers, and assorted community organizations, the trade union movement seems to have restrained itself to quiet lobbying and acquiescence to the neo-liberal agenda. In the midst of the current global economic crisis, BCers seem quiet as they await the promised 2010 Winter Olympic boom that is said to be coming. With massive drop in BC's resource sector revenue (upon which the province of BC relies) combining with the opening of most public sector labour contracts in the spring of 2010 (post-Olympics) quiescence is likely to turn into protest.

state funding had a disproportionately negative effect on CUNY where funding was already only 80% on a per student basis of the SUNY system.

These local particularities shaped the possibilities and dynamics of student activism. In B.C. the politics were class politics. In New York class politics were mediated through the lens of race. As a student engaged in militant political struggles there was a freedom of movement that is not possible as an employee of the university of excellence. However, as the next sequence of this paper discusses, new avenues of action emerge even as others are taken away.

In Struggle!

Radical posturing is easy to find within the pages of our academic community's journals, magazines, and newsletters. Anthropologists and their kindred colleagues seem able to muster righteous indignation over child labour in Latin America, inhumane and misogynist cultural practices in Africa, or even the barbarity of neo-colonialism practiced on indigenous peoples in 'our' backyards. But where is the everyday practice, the real social solidarity, that one might be excused for believing should accompany virtuous and radical sounding pronouncements in print?[14] This section of the paper explores the ways the structure of the academic workplace shapes and constrains the possibilities for progressive action.

Social Solidarity and the Academic Workplace[15]

So, why does the academic workplace engender a mode of social interaction that eschews social solidarity even when many of its practitioners publicly advocate what might loosely be termed a progressive politics? The academic workplace can be

---

14   I should hasten to add that not all academics engage in radical posturing – some are downright regressive in their outlook. Many academics find the competitive zero sum game of the academic pursuit of excellence perfectly acceptable. At the very least the honesty of those who find the system palatable in its current guise is admirable, if self-serving. What does stick in the craw, so-to-speak, is the ideological bafflegab produced by some academics and academic administrators who speak of collegiality on the one hand while they are busily engaged in undermining collaboration and solidarity on the other through their active support of market mechanisms. While of a different sort, the professional book radical is equally tiresome as they pronounce on conflicts and situations in far off places, produce volumes of radical sounding prose, but do nothing to make a real difference where they work and live.

15   To my colleagues who may misread the underlying sentiment as suggesting that there is in any way a personalized sense of grievance I want to set that aside right from the start. What I am talking about in this section is the structural aspect of our workplace and the ways in which the university of excellence militates against a full-fledged form of social solidarity. This is not to say that my immediate workplace environment lacks collegiality – it is a very collegial place to work. However, the social structure of the workplaces necessitates that gains by one end up being losses by another in terms of the economic and social status rewards within the workplace. So, to my dear friends and colleagues I ask that you read on understanding that this is a structural – not personal – critique.

described as one that is premised upon confrontational discourse and individual competitiveness in which career advancement is determined by individual gain in a zero sum game.

The material conditions of the academic work site do indeed have implications for how people interact with each other. My partner, who works in a public high school, often comments on the degree of collegiality and collaboration in her work place. Teaching resources are shared freely between colleagues. Ideas on how to manage classrooms and challenge students to learn are freely shared. Through these everyday communications and collaborations, a community of care and support is created. This degree of workplace solidarity extends beyond a focus on work and lies at the core of the militancy of teachers in the public schools system. Teachers in B.C. have a long history of job action that must in some important way draw on these everyday forms of collaboration and cooperation in their workplace.

Prior to my appointment at UBC in 1996 I worked in B.C.'s fishing industry as a commercial fisherman. The world of fisheries is one that requires social collaboration. Even at times when one may not like one's crewmates one must find ways to work together as the very physical requirements of work necessitates collaboration and cooperation in the work process. Working in close proximity with a small group of men under conditions where what I do affects the abilities of everyone else and vice versa leads to a social solidarity the likes of which I have never seen in the university of excellence. This is not to say that the world of fishermen or the world of public school teachers is an idyllic one of solidarity and bliss. What it is to say is that the structures under which individuals work shape and constrain their capacity to effectively collaborate, and that the world of a research university faculty member is one that is specifically orientated in a manner to undermine social solidarity in the workplace even as the ideology of collegiality is proclaimed.

Academic work is, in one sense, a form of glorified piecework. That is, we are rewarded by how much we produce. This is a deliberate and provocative claim. Clearly, most tenure stream faculty receive a base salary. University performance or merit pay systems are based on, among other things, publications. A friend recounts an anecdote in which their biology instructor explained to the class that each paper he published was valued at about $20,000 over his lifetime. He linked each published paper's value to merit pay and advancement through professorial ranks. He also suggested that it increased his capacity to negotiate individual salary increases. Many teaching-intensive post-secondary institutions have regulated pay scales. This is not, however, the case in research-intensive universities. For those of us working in research-intensive universities in countries such as Canada and the United States salary increases over and above standard career increases or general raises are individually negotiated. It is in this sense that I provocatively refer to academic labour as glorified piecework. I would add that while the situation in a North American research-intensive university may not be the normative case, it does set the criteria against which other forms of academic labour are measured.

Back to glorified piecework: as in any other workplace governed by piecework there is no fixed limit on what is expected. Of course, we implicitly understand that this is part of the university of excellence – we drive each other forward competing for scarce rewards of merit pay and advancement through the academic ranks knowing that if we slack off someone else might work harder. Those working outside of the research-intensive university rail against the teaching load that limits their ability to meet the publication goal required to gain access to the few privileged positions in the so-called 'top-tier' universities. It's an old trick that capitalists have used to inspire productivity, but it is always intriguing (and somewhat saddening) to watch how otherwise intelligent people internalize and argue for this dehumanizing work practice under the guise of excellence in scholarship.

Academics, like other professionals, have a fair degree of freedom in setting certain aspects of their conditions of employment. However, the hierarchical nature of tenure and promotion committees is such that effective control is placed within the hands of a relatively small group of academics at each institution, many of whom have participated in the management structure of their institutions as departmental chairs, program directors, deans, etc. While the system may vary from institution to institution the basic structure is similar. Tenure cases are reviewed first by a department (or equivalent) level committee of already tenured faculty. Their recommendation is passed up the administrative hierarchy to a Dean's (or equivalent) review committee that then sends its recommendation up to the final committee at the top administrative level of the institution. At each level in the process there is a committee of faculty and administrators of increasing seniority. The final decision normally rests with the institution's top academic administrator and approval by such board of governors or regents that may exist.

It is the peculiarity of our current workforce structure that, as jobs tightened in the 1980s and 1990s (and then again in the current period following a brief opening from the late 1990s to the 2007/8), following the 1960s/70s post-secondary expansion, hiring became more focused on actual rather than potential output. Thus, those hired during and up to the early 1980s were likely to be hired without PhD or publications. However, by the mid 1990s the going rate at UBC and similar universities of excellence was a minimum of three peer-reviewed publications at the point of hire. Since the late 1990s the focus has been on so-called 'top-tier' universities (which translates as American private or Ivy League universities) and, in the process, Canadian degrees become by definition sub-par (see, for example Silverman 1991)[16]

Progressive Action in the Workplace

The paradox of the university of excellence is that, in focusing on measurable output over the content of academic production, a space for progressive action is created. However, the focus on output over content can have some rather embarrassing, and in fact, fraudulent effects. Jan Hendrik Schön, "an up-and-coming physics and nanotechnology wunderkind" employed by Bell Laboratories managed to commit one of the largest hoaxes in recent times (Reich 2009:1). His falsified data were published in the 'top tier' science journals *Nature* and *Science* giving him the number two ranking globally according to the ISI Web of Science ratings for 2001; a clearly 'excellent' researcher by all measures of the day. His work was totally fabricated even if it was based on an idea that was eventually found to be correct. As science writer Eugenie Reich comments, the environment of competition for employment and advancement creates a climate in which fraud becomes possible "as almost all scientists, including those at universities, are working with the next grant application or major publication in mind, and it is not unheard of for researchers working on a project that is under threat to promote preliminary data more than they otherwise might" (2009:9).

The paradox of 'excellence' as an organizing principle is that it drives output rather than content. Here we can see a critical difference between the university of excellence and what Readings calls the university of 'culture' in which culture, tied to the project of the nation state, is the animating principle of the university (1996:62-118).[17] Within the university of culture what an academic said or published was more important than how much they said and published. In the university of culture the question of power was "structured in terms of the inclusion or exclusions of subjects from cultural participation" (Readings 1996:117). Thus, anthropologists who dissented during the US cold war lost their jobs for supporting anti-racist positions, not necessarily nor specifically for pro-communist positions (Price 2004). Intriguingly,

16   The preference for hiring non-Canadian Ph.D.s can be seen in a review of faculty in the 29 Canadian anthropology departments listed in the American Anthropological Association's 2009 guide to departments where 59% of faculty in Canadian departments offering a Ph.D. programme have non-Canadian degrees.
17   See also Price 2004 for a discussion of how the university of culture disciplined dissident anthropologists.

the primary threat to US capitalism and the cultural idea of Americanism in the 1950s and 1960s was (and, I would suggest, remains) racial equality. This likely arises from the ways in which race and class in the U.S. are intimately linked (Brodkin 2000, 1998, 1989). Thus, as long as academics in the university of excellence maintain their productivity at the rate being set by their colleagues a limited social space is opened up for progressive activity.

Putting Words into Action

Since my first appointment at UBC I have been involved in a number of local solidarity actions. Some have gone unnoticed by the university's administration; others have brought some minor criticism upon me.[18] I have also been involved in my community residents' association and, while my children were in school, in school-based parent advisory councils. All of these actions are fairly mainstream and 'normal' activities for many people in our society who also participate in civil society organizations. What has been different is my effort to locate my participation in efforts to democratize these various organizations and to build effective linkages between divergent groups on the basis of workplace organizations.

Early on in my employment at UBC the Asia Pacific Economic Co-operation (APEC) summit was held at UBC. The main events were housed at the university president's residence and the Museum of Anthropology – venues directly adjacent to my own office. A large community and student opposition to the event developed in the months leading up to the summit. The opposition was in part a reaction to the planned attendance of Indonesian dictator Suharto; but the more important point of opposition was the role that the APEC summit was playing in the global neo-liberal agenda. APEC was part of the international movement toward liberalized global trade and the consequent undermining of local economic security for working people.

Students and their allies ramped up their organizing and political protests as the university prepared for the coming world leaders. The fall 1997 protests at UBC became infamous in Canada for the actions of an RCMP office dubbed 'sergeant pepper' who sprayed protesters with pepper spray with little warning during one of

---

18 During the illegal 2005 public teachers strike I worked with two colleagues at UBC to organize a series of public demonstrations (one of which caused the university administration to send warning letters to faculty and support staff advising us that participation in the rally outside of lunch or coffee breaks would constitute an illegal withdrawal of labour) and a university forum (which caused a university administrator to send me series of late night emails advising me that I could not call the forum a UBC event unless my "career path" included related publications). See at: http://blogs.ubc.ca/newproposals/ 2005/11/teachers-strike-forum-videos/). In addition, with parent activists, I co-organized strike support activities at various schools throughout Vancouver including authoring a blog in support of public education.

several clashes between police and activists.[19] For those of us who had experience with political protests in the early 1980s, in which conflict with police had been common, the carnival-like performance of the No APEC protests seemed quite different. Student activists dressed up as clowns, beat on drums, and pirouetted their way toward police fences. The police responded with pepper spay and arrests. The protesters seemed surprised with the police response but continued to advance on the police. Many of the young protesters who had experience in the environmental movement were those who 'wanted' to be arrested; they marched toward some predefined line and were then peacefully arrested by the waiting police. The rough and tumble of police violence was a new experience for these student protesters who complained vociferously following their arrests. Nonetheless, the protests continued under the eyes of snipers perched on nearby buildings, police in riot gear, and undercover agents embedded in student protest organizations.

As a junior faculty member I didn't seem to realize that I should remain silent and stay out of trouble.[20] Drawing upon my then recent experience as a student activist and my understanding of the importance of having faculty support, I attempted to have our department take a formal position of opposition to the APEC leaders summit at UBC. However, my senior colleagues politely set the issue aside citing academic freedom as one justification not to take a position. Two senior colleagues later approached me. Each in their own way implied, rather than stated, that I should keep my head down during my pretenure period. Neither of them brought up the issue directly, but both visits were too close to the event at hand to really be understood as anything other than advice on how to survive in the academic workplace.[21] While I did not directly enter into the active protests I did, nonetheless, take up a role as witness to on campus protests during the summit as part of an ad hoc group of similarly minded faculty. The APEC lesson for me was that I needed to ensure that my activism was combined with academic output so that when my turn for review and promotion came up there would be enough 'output' to overshadow the 'deficiencies' of political activism.[22]

---

19   For a timely and thorough account see Andrew Larcombe's master's thesis "It was like the gauntlet was thrown down": the No! to APEC story (2000).

20   I am glad that I was not paralyzed by a false fear that some academics invoke by way of rationalizing their absence from political engagement. It is my sense that my life has been better for living my convictions than by trying to hide them.

21   It is likely that since my two senior colleagues had come of age within the university of culture, they were very much concerned that what a person said and published could have serious implications for career progress.

22   Constraints upon publishing and the mainstreaming of peer review publications toward the lowest common denominator of academic fashion is the subject of an entirely different paper. It is important to note

Over the course of the next decade or so I had many opportunities to put this lesson into practice. From support work for students who took over the university president's office in the mid-1990s through a series of protracted and at times bitter labour conflicts between the university and its various trade unions, I had many real-time opportunities to put words into action. During this period of time I also became involved in our university faculty association and had a first-hand experience of conservative unionism at work.[23] What became apparent to me is that being actively involved, even from a position of political dissent, is not in and of itself an obstacle to continued employment in Canada.

From my vantage point as a faculty member within the university of excellence, I can see the relative privilege that has been granted to us. We have a degree of freedom and flexibility that few other workers have. With this comes responsibility and obligations. If we wish to do more than simply participate in the reproduction of the dominant society and its attendant social inequities, then we have an obligation to go beyond radical words and directly involve ourselves in the democratic struggle in our work and communities. We need to be cautious to not act naively or without some form of wider support. We should, however, act. In what follows I outline some of the small ways that one can engage in progressive politics within and against the university of excellence.

New Proposals (Again!)

Kathleen Gough challenged anthropologists in 1968 to place their talents and personal political commitments behind the national liberation and anti-imperialist struggles of the day. Gough's call for new proposals are as relevant today as they were more than 40 years ago. As U.S., British, Canadian and other Western troops wage war in far-flung lands, workers in the heartland are confronting a resurgent

---

here that the pressures to only publish in, or to only count, so-called 'top-tier' (i.e. U.S.) journals as fitting measures of excellence is a growing problem. The net effect of these programs is a narrowing of publications in social science and humanities fields where faculty may self-censor and only publish what they think will be acceptable in the dominant U.S. journals. For colleagues who see their primary attachment as the imperial heartland this does not pose a significant problem. However, for those of us who see relevance in maintaining an autonomous Canadian tradition of scholarship this is a real problem that needs to be confronted.

23   Academic labourers, especially those of us in the university of excellence, often are quite supportive of systems of privilege and differential reward. Nonetheless, most of the people who were involved on the UBC Faculty Association during my three terms on the executive were dedicated scholars who found injustice and inequity in employment at UBC to be distasteful and they tried to address these imbalances. Despite the rather small 'c' conservative nature of the UBC faculty association, a slate with close ties to UBC's administration took control of the executive in 2007 on a platform of, among other things, rewarding excellence. Their major grievance was that the faculty association seemed to be anti-research and far too interested in supporting mediocre faculty then in building excellence. For the new executive, awarding excellence was the order of the day.

ruling class intent on dialing back any advance or advantage that working people have gained. As anthropologists our arena of struggle straddles the sites in which we conduct research and those in which we engage in teaching and writing. This duality should give us a unique purchase from which to engage in transformative politics. It is instructive to review the key points of Gough's argument before proceeding further.

New Proposals for Anthropologists: 1968

Anthropology is a child of Western imperialism. It has roots in the humanist visions of the Enlightenment, but as a university discipline and a modern science, it came into its own in the last decades of the 19th and the early 20th centuries. This was the period in which the Western nations were making their final push to bring practically the whole pre-industrial world under their political and economic control. [Gough 1968:403]

Gough goes on to describe how most anthropological research until World War II had been conducted in societies colonized by the West. In the years after World War II, this situation had begun to change as the majority of the colonized world achieved independence or was in the throes of anticolonial wars. Yet, this degree of political autonomy was threatened by an attempt by the U.S. government to re-impose Western power.

Western dominance is continuing under new guises, even expanding and hardening. At the same time, revolution now begins to appear as the route by which underdeveloped societies must hope to gain freedom from Western controls. [Gough 1968:405]

The question, says Gough, is "what does an anthropologist do who is dependent on a counter revolutionary government in an increasingly revolutionary world?" (1968:405). In answer to her own question Gough suggest two answers: anthropologists either become historians of small scale society or "admit that our subject matter is increasingly the same as that of political scientists, economists, and sociologists" (1968:405).

Anthropology, according to Gough, had failed to recognize that the world was a global system defined by imperialism (cf. Wolf 1982). Anthropologists had "virtually failed to study Western imperialism as a social system, or even adequately to explore the effects of imperialism on the societies ... studied" (1968:405). While noting several important exceptions (Eric Wolf and Peter Worsley among them) Gough comments "it is remarkable how few anthropologists have studied imperialism, especially the economic system" (1968:405). Those studies that have emerged often "assumed an international capitalist economy [without question] in its framework" (Gough 1968:406).

Gough concludes her essay with a short list of new research questions that would bring anthropology forward to face the realities of the world system and save the discipline from retreating from meaningful research. Each of her questions challenged anthropologists to put their skills to work to honestly evaluate the implications of imperialism for the world's majority populations.

> We should do these studies in our way, as we would study a cargo cult or Kula ring, without the built-in biases of tainted financing, without the assumption that counter-revolution, and not revolution, is the best answer, and with the ultimate economic and spiritual welfare of our informants and of the international community, rather than the short run military or industrial profits of the Western nations, before us. [1968:407]

Gough's call for a more relevant and engaged anthropology in 1968 was part of a movement in anthropology that was beginning to respond to the changing realities of fieldwork in former colonies. What have become commonplace concerns in today's anthropology were novel and even threatening to the discipline in 1968. Most anthropologists today highlight doing research that has meaning and value for the people being studied; most anthropologists try to be in some way collaborative and engage communities as partners in research; most anthropologists see themselves as in some way progressive, if only in a small 'l' liberal sort of way. Yet, when Gough called on the discipline to literally get their hands dirty working to make the world a better place, anthropology instead made a turn to literature and textual representations. Gough's concern with understanding and then transforming economic and political coercion in the then newly post-colonial transnational workplaces was set-aside in the competition for academic output in the university of excellence.

New Proposals for Anthropologists: 2010

Our workplace, the contemporary university of excellence, is at the forefront of neoliberal experiments and campaigns to target the most vulnerable and disadvantaged of the working classes. The university of excellence is governed by principles of accountability (emphasis on count) to the detriment of content, quality, or social equity. For example, class size limits are more likely to be set by national magazine report cards and related measures of excellence than by recourse to effective peda-gogy.[24] This is the context within which we produce papers, books, and conduct our research. It is also the terrain within which today's struggles for dignity and wellbe-ing is occurring. Our academic world is no longer (if it ever was) an isolated ivory tower. Our universities of excellence are at the core of the new world order. Our responsibilities and obligations thus call upon us to directly confront these forces in our workplace and through our actions.

First the practical concern: is there time to do all the things one needs to do to keep one's job (or to get one!) AND be actively engaged in progressive politics. As a parent of two who entered kindergarten in the same year I started working at UBC I say "yes there is time in the day!" However, the arena of struggle may shift.

For much of the last decade I was involved in my children's schools on parent advisory councils. Perhaps this is not so exciting as organizing demonstrations against dictators (as per the No APEC organizers) but, I would argue it is crucially important work just the same. One of the critical lessons taught by the old-line communist party union organizers in BC is that respect is built through everyday action. Networks developed through the everyday create the relationships that one is able to build from. These networks create the organizational base from which one can organize. These are the moments that have potential to make real change. As a parent I entered the world of my children's school and engaged in a politics aimed at democratizing and improving all children's learning experience. This involved activities from advocacy on behalf of other parents through to direct action in support of striking teachers. These are small 'r' reforms, but from these can come the capital 'R' revolutions in behaviours and society that will indeed usher in a better world for all.

As academics in the university of excellence, we are expected to win grants and publish papers. In this we have a lot of autonomy. I often say to my students: "Yes we must publish, but we get to choose what we publish."

For me this has led to a series of articles and films on research methods (2005, 2004, 2003, 2001a) in place of what I may have originally wished to publish. This shift reflects my concern for conducting ethical research and to resist the undue influence of the competitive drive to publish as much as one can. To me, a respectful research engagement means that one takes the time to consult and to work with the people about whom we write. Some researchers, lost in the competitive rush to

---

24   I was the chair of my department's undergraduate studies committee during a period when the Dean, having read a national news magazine report card on UBC class sizes, sent a directive to readjust course enrolment limits so that they meshed with the magazine's reporting structure. This allowed us to 'game the system' supposedly to boost our score on the national report card.

publish, prioritize their own advancement and desires over the people about whom they write. They do so without regard for consequence, seeking only the recognition that might come to them for rushing toward publication. It is possible to do honest, accurate, good work that is considerate of the people about whom we write; work that can contribute to making our world a better place. To do so should be an ethical and moral value to which we subscribe.

In our teaching we have an obligation and a responsibility to engage our students, to challenge them to examine and interrogate their values and their misconceptions of the world. This is not simply an activist pedagogy, it is a pedagogy based upon the principles of social justice and equality. It seems to me that learning in a context of social inequality, without understanding it or trying to do something about it, is an immoral act. Part of learning should mean learning about one's place in the world and the implications of privilege and disadvantage on our collective capacity to become fully human. Especially as anthropologists who actively engage people through our research and in our teaching, we have both a responsibility and an opportunity to put our words into actions that will create a better world for all.

Anthropology embodies a real possibility of transformative learning; but we need to take Gough's criticisms and proposals seriously in order to make good on the promise. What are the effects of global capitalism on people's health and wellbeing? How can we make democratic practice real and what does our knowledge of small-scale societies tell us about the possibility of true participatory democracy? Rather than studying those without power, can we renew the call to study up and focus on the ways in which local/ trans-national elites have gained control over public institutions such as the university of excellence? Wasting anthropological insight on interesting, but ultimately naïve and irrelevant topics, contributes to maintaining the status quo and thus is akin to complicity in the injustices of the global capitalist system.

From Action to Words to Action

I have spent three decades now involved in post secondary education: about half as a student and a bit more as a faculty member. Throughout this time I have had the occasion to observe first-hand the possibilities of progressive political engagement. Over this same period of time the nature of the global capitalist system has transformed, matured into a condition in which it is now clearly a global system that has subordinated the central components of all economies to the logic of capitalist accumulation. An anthropology that tries to cling to the partial study of small places or through the use of multiple local spaces while insisting upon the idea of the confluence of community and culture will indeed be relegated to the dustbins of history. Now, more than ever, our anthropological work – our social science work – AND our political work needs to be located fully "within a framework of understanding of what is happening to the larger system" (Gough 1968:405). Anthropology, as a politically engaged practice, has the capacity to turn ideas into actions that can create a better world for all of us.

References

Brodkin, Karen

    2000   Global Capitalism: What's Race Got to Do With It? American Ethnologist 27(2):237-256.

    1998   How Jews Became White Folks And What That Says About Race In America. Rutgers University Press.

    1989   Toward a Unified Theory of Class, Race, and Gender. American Ethnologist 16(3):534-550.

Callinicos, Alex

    1990   Against Postmodernism: A Marxist Critique. New York: St. Martin's Press.

Carrol, William and R.S. Ratner

    1989   Social Democracy, Neo-Conservatism and Hegemonic Crisis in British Columbia. Critical Sociology 16(1):29-53.

Coupland, Douglas

    1991   Generation X: Tales for an Accelerated Culture. New York: St. Martin's Press.

Crow, Daniel

    1999   From Protest to Powerlessness: A Marxist Analysis of the Ontario NDP. MA Thesis. Department of Politics. Brock University.

Galbraith, John Kenneth

    1998[1958] The Affluent Society. Boston : Houghton Mifflin.

Gough, Kathleen

    1968   New Proposals for Anthropologists. Current Anthropology 9(5):403-407.

Larcombe, Andrew

    2000   "It was Like the Gauntlet was Thrown Down": the No! to APEC story. MA Thesis. Department of Anthropology and Sociology. University of British Columbia.

Menzies, Charles R.

2005   Returning to Gitxaała. (video) Vancouver: Ethnographic Film Unit.

2004   Putting Words into Action: Negotiating Collaborative Research in Gitxaała. Canadian Journal of Native Education 28(1):15-32.

2003   The View from Gitxaała. (video). Vancouver: Ethnographic Film Unit.

2001a   Reflections on Research With, For, and Among Indigenous Peoples. Canadian Journal of Native Education 25(1):19-36.

2001b   Us and Them: The Prince Rupert Fishermen's Co-op and Organized Labour, 1931-1989. Labour/Le Travail 48:89-108.

1994   Stories From Home: First Nations, Land Claims, and Euro-Canadians. American Ethnologist 21(4): 776-791.

1992   On Permanent Strike: Class and Ideology in a Producers' Co-operative. Studies in Political Economy 38:85-108.

1990   Between the Stateroom and the Fo'c'sle: Everyday Forms of Class Struggle Aboard a Commercial Fishboat. Nexus 8(1):77-92.

Palmer, Bryan

1987   Operation Solidarity: the Rise and Fall of an Opposition in British Columbia. Vancouver: New Star Books.

Patterson, Thomas C.

2001   A Social History of Anthropology in the United States. New York: Berg.

Pfaff, Nicolle

2009   Youth Culture as a Context of Political Learning: How Young People Politicize Amongst Each Other. Young: Nordic Journal of Youth Research 17(2):167-189.

Price, David H.

2004   Threatening Anthropology: McCarthyism and the FBI's Surveillance of Activist Anthropologists. Durham: Duke University Press.

Przeworski, Adam

1985   Capitalism and Social Democracy. Cambridge: Cambridge University Press.

Ratner, R. S.

1998   Tracking Crime: A Professional Odyssey. In The Criminal Justice System: Alternative Measures, James Hodgson, ed. Pp. 101-134. Canadian Scholars Press: Toronto.

Readings, Bill

1996   The University in Ruins. Cambridge, Massachusetts: Harvard University Press.

Reich, Eugenie Samuel
    2009   Plastic Fantastic: How the Biggest Fraud in Physics Shook the Scientific World. New York: Palgrave Macmillian.

Silverman, Marilyn
    1991   Amongst 'Our Selves': A Colonial Encounter in Canadian Academia." Critique of Anthropology 11:381-394.

Quine, Thom
    1985   How Operation Solidarity Became Operation Soldout: How and Why the Union Bureaucrats Sold Out the 1983 Solidarity Movement. Toronto: International Socialists.

Wang, Xiaoying
    2005   Farewell to the Humanities. Rethinking Marxism 17(4):525-538.

Wolf, Eric R.
    1982   Europe and the People Without History. Berkeley: University of California Press.